AF624438

ADVANCED EDUCATIONAL ADMINISTRATION

ADVANCED EDUCATIONAL ADMINISTRATION

Edited by

Tara Chand
Ravi Prakash

KANISHKA PUBLISHERS, DISTRIBUTORS
NEW DELHI–110 002

KANISHKA PUBLISHERS, DISTRIBUTORS
4697/5-21A, Ansari Road, Daryaganj
New Delhi -110 002
Phones : 2327 0497, 2328 8285
Fax : 011-2328 8285
E-mail : kanishka_publishing@yahoo.co.in

Advanced Educational Administration
Edition: 2016
© Reserved

PRINTED IN INDIA

Published by Madan Sachdeva for Kanishka Publishers, Distributors, 4697/5-21A, Ansari Road, Daryaganj, New Delhi-110 002, Typeset by Sunshine Graphics, Delhi, and Printed at Rajdhani Printers, Delhi.

Preface

Public policy statements on vital indicators of development, such as, health, education, child development and family welfare have been welcome in recent years. They supplement, and in most cases, complement broad-based and generally focussed schemes, including Operation Blackboard, Literacy Mission, Health Cover for All by 2000, Navodaya Schools and others designed for the specific benefit of the millions of the country's poor, deprived, isolated and neglected masses. The efforts of planners and policy-makers has been motivated by the broad principles of the welfare state. Inputs need to be conceived, structured and channellised into the development mainstream. The present publication is a modest attempt in this direction.

It provides excellent framework for educational management and administration in the light of the new policies and plans for educational reform. The significant subjects covered are: policies and programmes of educational administration; defining democratic educational administration; administration and school management; management of educational plans and resources; financial resources for schools; statistics and record-keeping in administration; and personnel management and development. The publication will go a long way in filling a yawning gap in the related literature.

TARA CHAND
RAVI PRAKASH

Contents

1

The Definition of Administration

It has been estimated that there are at least 5,000,000 individuals in the United States today performing administrative work as their main function. At least 100,000 of these could be classified as holding major executive positions. This number is large, but as the technology and the specialized functions of this country advance, there will be an increasing number of individuals needed to perform the myriad administrative duties characteristic of the thousands of organizations in society. Administration offers many career opportunities for both women and men.

It is essential that individuals who perform administrative work know the many aspects of this particular field. If they are not aware of certain basic facts and are not acquainted with acceptable administrative procedures, many errors may be made. This could result in loss of efficiency, production, staff morale, and in poor human relations, to mention only a few of the possible outcomes. Administration is rapidly becoming a science with a body of specialized knowledge which should be known by all who would administer in a wise and effective manner. Plato in his book, *Laws*, summed it up in a few words which still hold true today: "... that God governs all things, and that chance and opportunity cooperate with Him in the government of human affairs. There is, however, a third and less extreme view, that art should be there also; for I should say that in a storm there must surely be a great advantage in having the aid of the pilot's art. You would agree?"

DEFINITION OF ADMINISTRATION

In an organization where the associated efforts of many individuals are necessary, there is no spontaneous and automatic working together of the individuals involved. There are no miraculous thought and planning which result in the achievement of goals and purposes. It is not a natural trait of human beings to cooperate and work side by side in a happy and purposeful manner. This is accomplished through direction, and administration gives this direction.

To a considerable degree, the actions of human beings in society are determined through their association with formal organizations. Formal organizations have leaders and purposes. They depend upon the cooperative efforts of individuals to achieve the objectives which have been set. Many times organizations have failed when their leaders have been of low calibre, there has been a lack of cooperative effort among members, or the objectives have not been in conformance with what is essential and good for society.

Administration determines in great measure whether an organization is going to progress, operate efficiently, achieve its objectives, and have a group of individuals within its framework who are happy, cooperative, and productive. It has to do with directing, guiding and integrating the efforts of human beings so that specific aims may be accomplished. It refers particularly to a group of individuals, many times called executives, who have as their major responsibility this direction, guidance, integration, and achievement.

Administration is especially concerned with achievement—proof that the organization is producing those things for which it has been established. To be able to achieve these results in a satisfactory manner presupposes an understanding of human relationships, and the ability to foresee the future and plan for any eventuality. It demands capacity to coordinate many different and conflicting types of human personalities. Good administration should insure that the associated efforts of individuals are productive. To accomplish this, administrators should possess those attributes which are conducive to bringing out the most creative and best efforts on the part of the members of the organization.

Administration also requires close supervision of the facilities, materials, supplies, and equipment essential to the life of the organization. It implies a logical formulation of policies and the effective operation of the organization.

In light of the above discussion, the author would like to propose as a definition of administration, the following:

Administration is concerned with the functions and responsibilities essential to the achievement of established goals through associated effort. It is also concerned with that group of individuals sometimes called executives. These individuals are responsible for directing, guiding, coordinating, and inspiring the associated efforts of individual members, so that the purposes for which an organization has been established may be accomplished in the most effective and efficient manner possible.

HISTORY OF ADMINISTRATION

Most of the facts concerning the history of administration have to do with public administration. To some, therefore, it may seem that they are not pertinent to the type of administration discussed in this book. However, it is well to remind the reader that this book has been written with the assumption there is certain basic knowledge which is applicable to all phases of administration whether it is associated with a church, school, public agency, government, or industry. Therefore, it is essential to examine all available administrative facts, whatever their specialized design.

The history of administration can be traced back as far as 1300 B.C., when the Egyptians were spreading their culture throughout the world. They had a system of large-scale administration. The decrees of Ramses III were recorded for history. The administrative setup of the Ptolemies provides some evidence of a systematic, though not always the most efficient, public administration. They had a planned economy with such work as industry, cattle breeding, and agriculture conducted along definite and prescribed lines.

The Byzantine Empire (330-1453) and the Ottoman Empire (1520-1566) under Suleiman contributed a system of civil service to administration.

Ancient Chinese records show that this people had a very good civil service system. They were aware that the public government had to abide by certain basic administrative principles.

The Greeks introduced democracy into administration when it placed government in the hands of all men. It recognized such basic facts as these: all men are equal before the law; a citizen should be interested not only in his own personal affairs, but also in the affairs of state; all citizens have a responsibility for deciding public policy; and full discussion of important public issues is an essential to good government.

The Romans showed their ability in large-scale management, which included the administration of their own affairs as well as the affairs of their subject colories. They established a paid system of civil service under Augustus about 25 B.C.

During the Middle Ages evidence points to considerable administrative thinking. The royal domains, ecclesiastical provinces, and feudal manors provided opportunity for various types of administrative practice. Local government administration was carried on by manor officials or ecclesiastical personnel. According to some historians and church people, the Catholic prelates and parish clergy could be given an excellent administrative rating in the light of present-day standards. Also, during the Middle Ages a fiscal procedure was developed for the Exchequer in England and additional administrative work was performed by such organizations as parliaments, synods, and councils.

A group of individuals to whom history owes much for their contributions to the science of administration were the Cameralists in Germany and Austria. The Cameralists were professors and public administrators whose work and influence have been traced back to around 1550. They were especially prominent during the 1700's. They were interested in scientific administration and did a great deal of work in connection with finance and other pertinent topics. They were scholars and applied their scholarship and practice to making administration a science.

During the eighteenth century, the formation of the United States Government stands out as the most important development in administration. It represents an attempt to devise a system of public government based on democratic principles. This great experiment attracted world-wide attention and many of its basic features have been copied by other peoples.

Woodrow Wilson, while at Princeton University, studied and wrote concerning the science of administration. Wilson recognized the importance of administration in government.

One of the outstanding developments of the twentieth century in the field of administration has been the stress placed upon scientific administration by industry. The industrial revolution pointed to the necessity for good organization and administration in order that industry might be most efficient and productive. Consequently, much literature has been published on the subject, educational institutions have initiated courses dealing with it, and more and more stress has been placed on the necessity for trained administrators.

The trend in industry has been contagious. All types of organizations, whether they relate to education, religion, government, or industry, are starting to recognize more and more the importance of administration as a science. These organizations realize the important part administration plays in achieving objectives which are essential to their success and to their ways of life and government. Teachers College, Columbia University, recently created a new Department of Educational Administration at a cost of $1,000,000, one which will cost $500,000 a year to operate. The purpose of this new department is to develop better principals, superintendents, and other school administrators. It is being increasingly recongized that administrative *savoir-faire* is most essential for the welfare of mankind.

Another development which has been much in evidence in recent years is the increased number of women in administrative positions. This is true of education, business, government, and all forms of endeavour. It is right that more women should occupy important administrative positions because qualifications are not restricted to one sex.

IMPORTANCE OF ADMINISTRATION

A study of administration is important for all individuals. A few of the more important reasons for such a study are listed here.

1. Administration is important in social, economic, political, religious, and educational affairs. It affects every person. The manner in which organizations are administered determines the course of men's lives. It affects their way of living, their goals, their ambitions, their happiness, and their achievements.
2. Administration will develop an understanding and an appreciation of a broad knowledge of the facts and practices which make up the science of administration as it is known today. Methods, techniques, devices, and procedures which are sound and in accordance with acceptable practice will be appreciated to a greater degree by all concerned.
3. A knowledge of administration will make it possible for the individual to recognize unsound practices in administration. Such a knowledge will help in restricting the exploitation of human resources and in furthering efficient management and organization.
4. A knowledge of administration will aid some individuals to decide whether or not to select this particular area on a career basis. It will aid them in evaluating their own qualifications for such work and help them to predict their own possibilities for success.
5. All administrative work is not confined to executives. Most employees and members of organizations outside the so-called executive or administrative group perform administrative duties. Even the head of family group performs administrative duties in connection with household and family management. Therefore, it is essential that all individuals possess an understanding and an appreciation of this work so that they may

efficiently carry out assignments. Furthermore, promotions and advancement often depend on one's knowledge of administrative technique.

6. Administration is fundamental in achieving joint purposes. Individuals are imbued with ideas which they want to see come to fruition. These ideas do not materialize unless there are planning and cooperative action. A knowledge of administration facilitates the achievement of such aims.
7. Administration helps to insure the continuance of organizations that have proved worthwhile to mankind and are needed in society. Its fundamental objective is to carry on that which has proved to be successful rather than to destroy the old and attempt a new and untried path.
8. A knowledge of administration furthers good human relations. Good administration implies cooperating with one another, being able to overlook personal shortcomings, getting along with people in order to obtain utmost work output and efficiency, and possessing the ability to instill the feeling of "one big happy family."

Outstanding individuals in various walks of like have recognized the importance of administration. Charles A. Beard, a famous historian, refers to administration as the key science of the present day. Henri Fayol, French engineer and industrialist, stresses the great need for studying administration scientifically, in that it is one of the most important elements in all vocations and professions. Paul Pigors, American sociologist, feels that the main contribution of administration is to preserve the *status quo* in society. Brooks Adams, American lawyer and historian, takes an almost opposite view from Pigors' when he advocates administration as being most important because it can help in social change. James Burnham, American political philosopher, goes further and points to the fact that the chief administrators in present-day society have assumed so much power that the social revolution is already in evidence. Charles E. Merriam, American political scientist, contends that administration is another outcome of human technology which is making it possible for man to better adapt to his complex environment.

The evidence is ample that administration is rapidly becoming a science and that the study of this science is essential to everyone. A study of administration can result in a better-ordered society, through more efficiently run organizations. Every individual belongs to formal organizations. Through a democratic approach to administration the individual can aid in carrying on what has proved to be good in the past and steer a course which will insure progress in the future.

QUALIFICATIONS OF THE ADMINISTRATOR

It is important that everyone recognizes the qualifications of a good administrator. This is essential to help determine whether or not one should go into this important field of endeavour if the occasion arises. It will also help in evaluating the type of administration one is experiencing in his own organization, whether he be an administrator or hold another position.

The qualifications of an administrator are many. A list of some follows. There has been no attempt to list these in order of importance, although in the discussion of each, one may be able to discern the most essential and important qualifications.

Important Qualifications

1. *Administrative Mind*

Some individuals have a capacity which, perhaps, has been developed through training and experience, and which peculiarly adapts them to administrative work. These individuals are able to analyze situations objectively, have the ability to clarify generalizations and possess the quality of administering in a constructive manner rather than in an exploitative way. Such persons are sensitive to human relations and the important part they play in the successful functioning of any organization. These individuals think in imaginative terms. They are able to see into the future and plan a course of action with an open mind. They recognize problems in order of importance, are able to analyze a situation, develop various plans of action, and reach logical conclusions. They have ability to organize. This is what is meant by an administrative mind, and it is not characteristic of all individuals. Instead, it is a part of the qualifications of comparatively few people. The persons who seem to have this capacity for administration should be identified and persuaded to assume administrative responsibilities because they have one of the primary requisities.

2. *Integrity*

One of the most important qualifications of any administrator is integrity. Whether or not a leader can inspire the staff, have their cooperation, and achieve purposes of the organization will depend to a great degree upon his or her integrity. Everyone likes to feel that an administrator is honest and sincere, keeps promises, can be trusted with confidential information, and is an individual in whom one has faith. Such confidence cannot emanate from administrators unless they have integrity. Failure to fulfil this one qualification will result in low morale and an inefficient organization.

3. *Ability to Instill Good Human Relations*

The ability to get along with associates in work is an essential qualification for an administrator. Only through cooperative efforts is it possible for an organization to achieve its goals. This cooperative effort is greatest when the individuals responsible for coordination of human efforts have the welfare of the various members of the organization at heart. This means that an administrator must be able to convert the abilities of many individuals into coordinated effort. This is done in many ways. Some of these methods include setting a good example, inspiring confidence, selecting proper incentives, possessing poise, making the right decisions in tense moments, having an impersonal attitude, cooperating and helping others when necessary, and developing and practising ethical standards. The administrator must be adept at the art of persuasion, which takes into considerations such important items as the points of view, interests, and other factors characterizing those to be persuaded.

There is very little associated effort without leadership. The administrator must be a leader and possess the attributes and qualities which people expect if they are to follow and contribute their best to achieve the purposes for which the organization has been established.

4. *Ability to Make Decisions*

The administrator must be able to make decisions when the situation necessitates such action. This presumes an understanding of what constitutes the important and the unimportant in the particular situation that is in question, the ability to foresee future developments and results of a decision, and a knowledge of what is reasonable and what is unreasonable. It also assumes knowledge as to what is in the best interests of the organization and what is not, and what has the best chance for success and what has the least chance.

Decision is essential in order to accomplish objectives at the most opportune time. The administrator should have the capacity and be willing to make a decision. Many times if a decision is not forthcoming lethargy, suspense, and poor morale are created. The cooperative process depends upon decisions being made. It is absolutely necessary to insure decision throughout the entire organization so that one can experiment in new and better ways of doing things and adapt successfully to changing conditions. The administrator who procrastinates beyond a reasonable time, is afraid of making the wrong decision, thinks only of his or her own security, and is oblivious to the organization's needs should never hold such a position.

5. *Health and Fitness for the Job*

Good health and physical fitness are essentials for the administrator. Good health and physical fitness often have a bearing on making the right decisions. Socrates once said that people in a state of bad health often made the wrong decisions in regard to affairs of state. Jennings, the famous biologist, pointed out that the body can attend to only one thing at a time. Therefore, if attention is focused on a pain in the chest, a stomach ailment, or a nervous condition, it is difficult to focus it on the functions which an administrator must perform. Poor health may cause poor administration.

Vitality and endurance are essential to the administrator. They affect one's manner, personality, attractiveness, and disposition. Administrative duties often require long hours of tedious work under the most trying conditions. Failure to have the necessary strength and endurance under such conditions could mean inability to perform tasks which are essential to the welfare of the organization. Members of an organization have confidence in those administrators who watch over their interest under all conditions. It is possible for an adminstrator to obtain this confidence continuously only if he or she is in good health and physically fit to perform arduous duties.

When considering health and fitness for the job, it is important to recognize the many phases of health. The administrator should possess not only physical, but also mental, emotional, and social health. Emotional stability, especially, is a must.

6. *Willingness to Accept Responsibility*

Every administrator must be willing to accept responsibility. There are duties to be performed which greatly influence the welfare of many individuals. Plans have to be fulfilled if the purposes of the organization are to be accomplished. Action is required to insure production and render services. The person who accepts an administrative job is morally bound to assure the responsibility that is part and parcel of that position. A good administrator will experience a feeling of dissatisfaction whenever he fails to meet responsibilities.

7. *Understanding of Work*

The administrator will benefit from having a thorough understanding of the specialized work in which the organization is engaged. If it concerns a particular industry, it will be an advantage to know the production process from the ground up. If it is government, knowledge of related legislative, executive, and judicial aspects will help. If it is education, being thoroughly familiar with that particular field will be an asset. If it is a specialized field within education or other areas, it is necessary to have a knowledge of the particular speciality and also the part it plays in the whole process. It is difficult to guide purposefully and intelligently unless the technical knowledge is present, together with an understanding of its relation to the activities and situations with which it is concerned. One often reads about the Congressman who started as a page in the Senate, the railroad executive who once was a yard worker, the bank president who started as a bookkeeper, and the superintendent of schools who many years before started as a teacher. The technical knowledge and understanding of the total functioning of an organization are best gained through firsthand experience. An administrator will find that detailed knowledge of an organization's work is of great help in successfully guiding its operations.

8. *Command of Administrative Technique*

Administrative technique in many ways is similar to the first qualification listed, namely, "administrative mind." There is one essential difference. "Administrative mind" refers more to the "knowhow" and temperament of the individual, whereas "administrative technique" refers to the application of this knowledge and ability. It means that the individual can plan and budget his or her time and effort and also the time and work of others, in the most effective way possible. Time is not spent on details when more important work should be done. Tasks are performed in a relaxed, efficient, calm, and logical manner. Work is accomplished in conformance with established standards. Duties are effectively executed, including those which involve strong pressure and great amounts of time. Resources for performing the job are utilized.

It has been said there are three conditions which burn out an administrator in a short length of time: performing his own duties in a tense, highly emotional manner, performing too many details, and being part of an organization which is not considerate of its administrators.

9. *Intellectual Capacity*

Intellectual capacity in itself will not guarantee a good administrator. In fact, the so-called "intellectual" often makes a very poor administrator. Such traits as absent-mindedness and non-punctuality are not compatible with acceptance of responsibility. The "intellectual" sometimes cannot make decisions because he visualizes so many sides of an issue. Furthermore, such an individual is often not interested in people, but in books, figures, or other data instead. This makes a poor leader since lack of interest in human beings results in poor followership.

However, one should not gain from this discussion that intellectual capacity should be disregarded. To be a good administrator one must be intellectually competent. One should be able to think and reason logically, to apply knowledge effectively, to communicate efficiently, and he should possess other factors which are closely allied to the intellectual process. There have been many so-called "brains" who failed miserably as administrators, whereas most good administrators can usually be classified as at least average in respect to their intellectual capacities.

Space has not permitted a discussion of all the qualifications of the administrator. Others, such as courage and initiative, are also important. There is also the ability to be an "ambassador" for the organization. Liaison work with higher echelon groups in organization and also with outside groups is important. It is necessary at times to stand up and fight for one's own department or division. To a great degree this will determine whether it is respected and on an equal basis with other administrative divisions.

WHY ADMINISTRATORS FAIL

The previous section has indicated the qualifications that are needed for administrative success. According to one of the outstanding business publications the following are the principal reasons why administrators fail:

1. Too many listen only for what they want to hear.
2. Too many fail to create a genuinely permissive atmosphere in which the subordinate feels free to express himself frankly and completely.
3. Too many fail to recognize that their real strength rests not in themselves but in the people they manage.

4. Too many permit distractions, petty irritations and prejudices to divert them from the main track in the discussion of business problems with their associates and subordinates.
5. Too many fail to recognize the need for getting an employee's complete participation.
6. Too many pay only lip service to the principle of two-way communication.

CHECK LISTS FOR ADMINISTRATORS

Such outstanding business firms as General Electric, Standard Oil of New Jersey, General Foods, Westinghouse, and many others are using check lists to evaluate their executives. These traits that are rated are valuable to any individual, whatever organization he may administer. One of America's largest corporations grades its executives on the following, classifying them in each case as very satisfactory, satisfactory, or unsatisfactory:

Dependability	Self-expression
Stability	Health and vitality
Imagination	Ability to plan and control
Originality	Cooperation

The National Office Management Association recently distributed approximately 20,000 forms to employees in companies across the country. These forms were questionnaires requesting from employees the answer to the question "What makes a good supervisor?" The tabulation of answers indicated that the following might be a good check list for the interested executive:

1. The good executive keeps his people informed about what's going on in the office.
2. A display of energy was the last of sixteen desirable characteristics of an executive.
3. Failure to recognize good work, especially among older employees, is a major complaint among employees.

4. Formal education ranked very low as a desirable characteristic of executives.
5. A good executive sees that justice is done to everyone.
6. Swearing is one of the least irritating qualities of executives.
7. Male supervisors are preferred.
8. Twelve qualities are more irritating than a display of temper in front of employees.
9. Supervisors who are near the age brackets of the people under them are preferred.
10. Very few employees listed a sense of humour among the first five characteristics preferred in executives.
11. A first name basis was preferred by employees in addressing executives.

THE ADMINISTRATOR'S DILEMMA

The following humorous statement has come to the attention of the author. It is passed along to the reader as a means of portraying some of the difficulties the administrator faces in his job.

THE ADMINISTRATOR'S DILEMMAS

If he's late for work in the morning, he is taking advantage of his position.
If he gets to the office on time, he's an eager beaver.
If the office is running smoothly, he's a dictator.
If the office is a mess, he's a poor administrator.
If he holds weekly staff meetings, he is in desperate need of ideas.
If he doesn't hold staff meetings he doesn't appreciate the value of teamwork.
If he spends a lot of time with the boss, he's a backslapper.
If he's never with the boss, he's on his way out.
If he goes to conventions, he's on the gravy train.
If he never makes a trip, he's not important.
If he tries to do all the work himself, he doesn't trust anybody.
If he delegates as much as possible, he's lazy.

If he tries to get additional personnel, he's an empire builder.
If he doesn't want more employees, he's a slavedriver.
If he has lunch in expensive restaurants, he's putting on the dog.
If he brings his lunch to the office, he's a cheapskate.
If he takes his brief case home, he's trying to impress the boss.
If he leaves the office without any homework, he has a sinecure.
If he's friendly with the office personnel, he's a politician.
If he keeps to himself, he's a snob.
If he makes decisions quickly, he's arbitrary.
If he doesn't have an immediate answer, he can't make up his mind.
If he works on a day-to-day basis, he lacks foresight.
If he has long-range plans, he's a daydreamer.
If his name appears in the newspapers, he's a publicity hound.
If no one has ever heard of him, he's a non-entity.
If he requests a larger appropriation, he is against economy.
If he doesn't ask for more money, he's a timid soul (or stark mad).
If he tries to eliminate red tape, he has no regard for system.
If he insists on going through channels, he's a bureaucrat.
If he speaks the language of public administration, he's a cliche expert.
If he doesn't use the jargon, he's illiterate.
If he writes for the Public Administration Review, he's neglecting his work.
If he has never written an article, he hasn't had a thought of his own in twenty years.
If he enjoys reading this, he's facetious.
If he doesn't think it's funny, he is entitled to his own opinion.

MAJOR ADMINISTRATIVE DUTIES

Gulick and Urwick have utilized the word POSDCORB to outline the functions of an administrator. This is based on Henri Fayol's work, *Industrial and General Administration.* An organization of duties under these major headings is apropos to the section under discussion. POSDCORB refers to the functional elements of (1) Planning, (2) Organizing, (3) Staffing, (4) Directing, (5) Coordinating, (6) Reporting, and (7) Budgeting.

Planning

Planning is the process of outlining the work that is to be performed, in a logical and purposeful manner, together with the methods that are to be utilized in the performance of this work. The total plan will result in the accomplishment of the purposes for which the organization is established. Of course this implies a clear conception of the aims of the organization.

In order to accomplish this planning, the administrator must have vision to look into the future and prepare for what he sees. He must see the influences which will affect the organization and the requirements that will have to be met.

Organizing

Organizing refers to development of the formal structure of the organization whereby the various administrative coordinating centres and subdivisions of the work are arranged in an integrated manner, with clearly defined lines of authority. The purpose behind this structure is the effective accomplishment of established objectives. Organizational charts aid in clarifying such organization.

This formal structure should be set up in a manner which avoids red tape and provides for the clear assignment of every necessary duty to some responsible individual. Whenever possible, standards should be established for acceptable performance for each duty assignment.

The coordinating centres of authority are developed and organized chiefly on the basis of the work to be done by the organization, services performed, individuals available in the light of incentives offered, and efficiency of operation. A single administrator cannot perform all the functions necessary, except in the smallest organizations. Hence, responsibility must be assigned to others in a logical manner. These individuals occupy positions along the line, each position being broken down in terms of its own area of specialization. The higher up the line one goes, the more general is the responsibility; the lower down the line one goes, the more specific is the responsibility.

Staffing

The administrative duty of staffing refers to the entire personnel function of selection, assignment, training, and providing and maintaining favourable working conditions. The administrator must have a thorough knowledge of the staff. He or she must select with care and insure that each subdivision in the organization has a competent leader and that each employee is assigned to the job where he can be of greatest service. Personnel should possess energy, initiative, and loyalty. The duties of each position must be clearly outlined. All members of the organization must be encouraged to utilize their own initiative. They should be rewarded fairly for their services. The mistakes and blunders of employees must be brought to their attention and dealt with accordingly. Vested interests of individual employees must not be allowed to endanger the general interests of all. The conditions of work should be made as pleasant and as a nearly ideal as possible. Both the physical and social factors should be provided for. Services rendered by the individual increase as the conditions under which he works improve.

Directing

Directing is a responsibility which falls to the administrator as the leader. He or she must direct the operations of the organization. This means distinct and precise decisions must be made and embodied in instructions which will insure their completion. The administrator must direct the work in an impersonal manner, avoid becoming involved in too many details, and see that the organization's purpose is fulfilled according to established principles. Executives have a duty to see that the quantity and quality of performance of each employee are maintained.

The administrator is a leader. His or her success is determined by ability to guide others successfully toward established goals. Individuals of weak responsibility and limited capability cannot perform this function successfully. The good administrator must be superior in determination, persistence, endurance, and courage. He must clearly understand his organization's purposes and keep them in mind as he guides and leads the way. Through direction, it is essential that faith be created in the cooperative enterprise, in success, in achievement of personal ambitions, in integrity of the leadership provided, and in the superiority of associated efforts.

Coordinating

Coordinating means interrelating all the various phases of work within an organization. This means that the organization's structure must clearly provide for close relationships and competent leadership in the coordinating centres of activity. The administrator must meet regularly with chief assistants. Here arrangements can be made for unity of effort, reports can be submitted on progress, and obstacles to coordinated work can be eliminated. Good coordination also means that all factors must be considered in their proper perspective.

This duty requires the establishment of a faith which runs throughout the organization. Coordination can be effective only if there is faith in the enterprise and in the need for coordinated effort. It is the motivating factor that stimulates human beings to continue rendering service so that goals may be accomplished.

There should also be coordination with administrative units outside the organization where such responsibilities are necessary.

Reporting

Reporting is the administrative duty of supplying information to administrators or executives higher on the line of authority or to other groups to which one is responsible. It also means that subordinates must be kept informed through regular reports, research, and continual observation. In this respect the administrator is a point of intercommunication. In addition to accepting the responsibility for reporting to higher authority, he must continually know what is going on in the area under his jurisdiction. Members of the organization must be informed on many topics of general interest, such as goals to be achieved, progress being made, strong and weak points, and new areas proposed for development. This information will come from various members of the organization.

Budgeting

As the word implies, budgeting refers to financial planning and accounting. It is the duty of the administrator to allocate to various subdivisions the general funds allotted to the organization. This must be done in a manner which is equitable and just. In carrying out this function, he must keep the organization's purposes in mind and apportion the available money to those areas or projects which will help most in achieving these purposes. It also means controls must be established to insure that certain limits will be observed, so-called "budget padding" will be kept to a minimum, and complete integrity in the handing of all the budgetary aspects of the organization will be maintained.

Fayol's Administrative Duties

A list of sixteen administrative duties in Gulick and Urwick's book, *Papers on the Science of Administration,* has been credited to Fayol, a specialist in administration. They are worthy of careful thought by all who are in or who covet administrative positions, since they reflect considered opinion of a few years back.

1. See that the plan of operations is carefully prepared and strictly carried out.
2. See that the human and material organizations are suitable for the objects, resources, and needs of the undertaking.
3. Establish a management which is competent and has a singleness of purpose.
4. Coordinate operations and efforts.
5. Make decisions which are clear, distinct, and precise.
6. Make careful selection of staff—each department has a competent and energetic head: each employee where he can be of most service.

7. Define duties clearly.
8. Encourage the desire for initiative and responsibility.
9. Reward men fairly and judiciously for their services.
10. Impose penalties for mistakes and blunders.
11. See that discipline is maintained.
12. See that individual interests do not interfere with the general interest.
13. Pay special attention to unity of command.
14. Ensure material and human order.
15. Subject everything to control.
16. Avoid red tape.

The duties of the administrator that have been discussed above show how essential his work is to the maintenance and effectiveness of any organization. He or she has the responsibility of maintaining the organization by leading a group of individuals toward the accomplishment of specified goals.

CODE FOR ADMINISTRATORS

Francis J. Curtis, Vice-President of the Monsanto Chemical Company, pointed out recently in a speech that administrators should be protected from overwork. He emphasized this point by stating that a man 47 years old who had started his business career at 22 at a salary of $3,600 and had advanced to the second echelon from the top management post and a salary of $40,000 was worth to the company, at the very least $425,000. He laid down for executives ten requirements for membership in what he called the *Coronary Club*. These rules were as follows:

1. Your job comes first; personal considerations are secondary.
2. Go to the office evenings, Saturdays, Sundays, and holidays.
3. Take the brief case home on the evenings when you do not go to the office. This provides an opportunity to review completely all the troubles and worries of the day.
4. Never say no to a request—always say yes.

5. Accept all invitations to meetings, banquets, committees, etc.
6. Do not eat a restful relaxing meal—always plan a conference for a meal hour.
7. Fishing and hunting are a waste of time and money—you never bring back enough fish or game to justify the expense. Golf, bowling, pool, billiards, cards, gardening, etc., are a waste of time.
8. It is a poor policy to take all the vacation time that is provided for you.
9. Never delegate responsibility to others—carry the entire load at all times.
10. If your work calls for traveling, work all day and drive all night to make your appointment for the next morning.

The value of administrator to his organization should be recognized and the necessary measures provided to protect the investment. Mr. Curtis felt that able assistants, regular medical examinations, compulsory vacations, sabbatical leaves, retirement provisions, hobbies, and outside interests were some essential measures.

2

Principles for Administration

Administration is the process of managing an enterprise so that the purposes of those engaged in it may be achieved. This function applies whether the enterprise is large or small, simple or complex. Usually specialized services will be needed and, often, rather complicated organizational structure set up to achieve it. In no case should the services or the structure become ends in themselves. Administration exists to serve the group. Administration is the specialized service of the organization designed to "oil the machinery", to make it possible for the purposes established by the group to be achieved.

The task of administration is complicated and highly diverse. It must recognize both the direct and indirect influences of factors which it alone can control. The inter-relationships of principle and objectives and the climate of permissiveness which it is the responsibility of administration to invoke represent the foundation stones upon which will be built effective or ineffective operational structure. No specialization is more important in any organization than this area of administration. The fortunes of the whole educational enterprise are dependent on the skill and competence, the vision and imagination, the integrity and quality of the administrative leadership.

FUNCTION OF ADMINISTRATION

The social heritage of Americans is a vast system of achievements, beliefs, and traditions, some of which were once the cherished visions of a few individuals. These elements—modified, perfected, and interwoven—now constitute the foundations of our culture. Each new generation is trained to respect and support the heritage and education interprets and transmits the values which underlie it, sometimes challenging, sometimes inspiring change. The manner in which the innovations of yesterday become fixed and patterned is principally the result of organization and management. An idea does not institutionalize itself. It is the function of administration to give it structure and to implement it.

It is the administrative function, therefore, that insures the continuance of existing order. Its fundamental aim is to "carry on". Organizations that are vital and dynamic have research and experimental divisions to venture on new and untried paths. But these paths are not undertaken until their worth has been proved. Administrators are the stabilizers of society.

Such stabilization has both a negative and a positive aspect. Administrators not only make possible the continuance of the ideas which they convert into institutions; they also frustrate many innovations to which they deny their support. They test each new development with a view to its effect on established interests. But in resisting change they slow down the rate of experimentation so that the main body of society can keep pace with it. The ponderous social machinery which is so irritating to the impulsive initiator is thus a safeguard against sudden changes which would paralyze the less adaptable members of society and which would bring chaos if not subjected to organizational checks.

DEMOCRATIC ASPECTS OF ADMINISTRATION

There are various levels of quality in the relations between the specialized groups which constitute an organization, various degrees in which they attain democratic interaction. Little democratic quality exists when the management is centered in a few individuals who have authority to make and execute policies after only limited consultation with those who must live under such policies. A greater degree of democratic quality exists when members manage an enterprise cooperatively. Administration that is democratic is thus an integral part of the efforts of groups to study their problems together, the delegate responsibility and work cooperatively toward the achievement of goals which they have agreed to share.

So it is that, while administration crystallizes and checks individual experiments, it must also permit the organization to be continuously revitalised by the spirit of freedom for initiative or it soon becomes obsolete and out of touch with the changing order. It is in this way that administration that is democratic enriches and invigorates its organization. By a structure of patterns which allow for participation on the part of the member groups, rich stores of individual initiative are tapped, and the group enterprise is more vibrant and effective because of it.

It is helpful to think of administration in terms of an inherent complementary pattern that exists between the following:

good will	and	good methods
attitude	and	structure
intention	and	performance
motive	and	mechanism

If the mental sets in the first column are ever to be brought out of the realm of wish into tangible reality, the translation must be achieved through the function of administration. The mental outlook always has to be implemented to be effective, and the quality of this aspect is dependent on the structure that provides the means for its development into performance.

Good intentions without techniques for implementation "never get off the ground". Dewey makes the point in this fashion. He says that the principle of magic is invoked whenever it is hoped that results will be achieved without intelligent control over the means, or when it is supposed that means can exist and yet remain inert and inoperative. The means that are employed fashion the ends that will be achieved.

When this fact is applied to the administrative procedure it will be seen that democracy cannot be attained until its working principles are more fully utilized in the means and ways of working. More specifically, organizations cannot adequately achieve regard for the dignity of man until they have moved through enough processes which permit the uniqueness of each individual to be expressed. Similarly, they must underline the process involved in each and every element of democracy which can be identified. Thus by vitalizing the means, organization more clearly realize ends. Administration is the tool, the instrument which creates the programme, the machinery by which things happen. Administration must reflect the purposes of the programme and have no values different from them. Administration is the agent through which purpose and philosophy achieve vitality and consummation.

ATTRIBUTES OF A GOOD ADMINISTRATOR

It is important that everyone recognize the attributes of a good administrator. For some, such recognition will be helpful as they work toward the acceptance of administrative responsibility. For others, for all staff members, this recognition will be an aid in evaluating the type of administration under which one works and in appreciating both the strengths and weaknesses of the organization. No attempt is made to list attributes in any particular order. Each is important in its contribution to total competence.

Ability to Make Decisions

The ability to make decisions calls for an understanding of the relative importance of issues, of timing, of public relations. The administrator must have a knowledge of relationships and a sense of perspective. The ability to foresee the eventual results of a decision of minor importance in the possible eventualities for tomorrow is an important attribute.

Willingness to Accept Responsibility

Closely related to the ability to make decisions, the attribute of willingness to accept responsibility is essential in an administrator. No one can be right all the time. The person who hesitates, who must be positive he is right before he decides, should not accept administrative responsibilities. Willingness to be on the firing line; to accept criticism, often unjust and unkind; to accept duties which concern to welfare of many; to carry heavy burdens and never be free of their load—these are requirements for an administrator. The ability to accept responsibility when the circumstances require decision and action, as opposed to the inclination to follow the easier part, "to wait and see what breaks", separates those who may be good administrators from those whose aptitudes are better utilized in other ways.

Ability to Work with Others

Needless to say, the ability to get along with one's associates is a prerequisite to good administration. It takes cooperation to help a group or organization achieve its purposes, and the administrator must be able to develop and maintain rapport with those with whom he works.

Integrity

Closely associated with the ability to work with others is the essential integrity of the leader. Knowledge of his sincerity, his honesty of purpose, his faith in the task and in his associates is the basis for confidence and cooperation on the part of his colleagues. Confidence is built on integrity, and without it no administrator can succeed.

Stability

It takes vitality and endurance to control one's disposition, restrain the rising temper, maintain good humour, and be patient in the face of tedious and trying circumstances. Emotional stability is essential. Important decisions, fateful conferences, the handling of a delicate situation cannot wait until the administrator feels ready to face them. They must be met under conditions of tension or tiredness, with the energy of the moment. Good staying power is very important.

Willingness to Be of Service

The function of administration implies a willingness to be of service. The administrator helps to create the atmosphere, the environment wherein others must work. He solves problems so that others may work up to their potential, in circumstances which are conducive to maximum creative endeavour. He has the task of encouraging, stimulating, and inspiring those who are members of the organization. Essentially it is a service role.

DUTIES OF AN ADMINISTRATOR

The necessities for administration grow with the magnitude of the task. When the number of special assignments multiplies and increasing numbers of people are involved there is a need to coordinate effort in order to utilize the unique skills of each to best advantage. Responsibilities need to be divided because, as Nash says, "Men differ in nature, capacity and skill, and gain greatly in dexterity by specialization; the same man cannot be in two places at the same time; one man cannot do two things at the same time; and, the range of knowledge and skill is so great that a man cannot within his life-span know everything or be proficient in all aspects of a situation." In other words, a division of work involves a consideration of human nature, and of time and space. The roles of authority in one realm confer no sovereignty in another. Because a man is expert in one area it does not necessarily follow that he is an authority in others.

So the duties of an administrator become a specialized phase of the total organization. Such duties have been variously categorized. Planning, organizing, staffing, budgeting, reporting, directing may be considered the major areas.

Broadly conceived, administration has three main functions: legislative, executive, and supervisory. Legislative function is concerned with policy formation, with planning and organizing, with rules and regulations. Executive function is concerned with staffing and directing the organization, delegating authority, financial planning and accounting, and the reporting aspects of liaison between members of the organization higher and lower in the line of authority. Supervisory function is concerned with in-service training, conference and coordination.

The principles for administration cut across each of these functions and can be discussed in terms of guides for action in the areas of personnel relationships and programme organization and operation.

PRINCIPLES FOR PERSONNEL RELATIONSHIPS

Responsibility

Responsibilities of the Various Duties of Personnel must be Clearly Defined

In the modern age of specialization the programme requires utilization of the unique skills of many. Diverse interests and diverse competencies exist. It is important therefore that the director divide the various duties among the staff members. Clearly defined and exact duties will prevent misunderstandings, duplication of work and jealousy and ill-feeling that might arise regarding imagined or real conflict in terms of overlapping responsibilities.

Authority

Delegated Authority and Responsibility must Carry Commensurate Authority and Power

The assignment of duties must carry with it the freedom for initiative and the responsibility for assumption of credit or blame for the end results. There is a framework of limitations which should be clearly established with the delegation of duties. Within this framework, the individual needs to be given the authority to proceed to carry out his assignment. The administrator who assigns tasks without commensurate authority to carry them out ties the hands of his associates and creates a situation bound to be fraught with trouble and dissent.

Esprit de Corps

The Loyalties of All must be to a Whole Greater than the Sum of the Parts

Each staff member will have some unique and special responsibilities. Those who specialize need to see their part in perspective and to have loyalty to that whole which is beyond the units with which they work. Each belongs to an organization and to its purpose he contributes. The whole is greater than the sum of the units. It is the function of administration to assign to individual members, in addition to duties in his area of specialization, responsibilities which will help each to see this relationship and to develop an understanding and appreciation for the larger whole. Vested interests, political influences, entrenched prejudices, jealousy, and bickering are the arch-enemy of cooperative achievement. They must be tampered with all the skill and diplomacy that can be developed on the part of the administrator.

Representation

Those Affected by the Policies of an Organization should Share in the Formulation of such Policies

Implementation of this principle requires that members shall have representation on the councils where administrators perform their legislative function. Within this framework staff members should participate in administrative work, and management should insure each special interest group adequate representation on policy-forming councils. Here a small working group provides a structure wherein secure and practical judgments can be formed and basic policy standards developed for the entire organization.

It should be noted that the democratic principle of representation limits the participation of staff members to these policy-forming, advisory functions. The executive aspects in the implementation of policy are the prerogative of the administrator.

Group Process

The Application of the Techniques of the Group Process in Personnel Relationships should be Incumbent upon those Who Accept the Democratic Method

The techniques of the group process are but implementing devices based upon certain principles designed to achieve the development of cooperation and consensus where groups of individuals work together to achieve common purposes. Stuart Chase, in *Roads to Agreement*, identifies five standards which are basic to the development of group consensus: participation, group energy, clearing communication lines, presentation of facts, and the development of a sense of security.

Regarding participation, he makes the point that the keynote is doing things *with* people, not *to* them. Administrators who can involve staff members in a procedure to which their loyalty is solicited because they sense their share of the responsibility for the accomplishment of common goals develop *esprit de corps* far superior to that achieved by autocratic command. People who work together can transcend the achievement of people who work for others.

The keynote of harnessing group energy is the permissive structure which provides for the release of this energy. Group energy is not a myth. It can be seen at work destructively in the power of mob violence. It can be seen at work constructively in conference when the sheer will of the group achieves something more than one man could have achieved alone. Within well-defined limits, group energy when directed and focused by leadership can be a powerful force for achievement.

The third standard, clearing of communication lines, is vital because little, if anything, can be achieved without communication. It is the task of leadership to recognize the elements which close the lines of communication and the techniques which help to keep them open. Problems in interpersonal relations, misunderstandings growing out of the difficulties of exact meaning and usage of words, bias and prejudice related to race, creed and religion—all these can snarl the lines and make cooperation and good will disappear in a flash. Group consensus is impossible when the members of a group cannot understand one another. Patience and skill in the techniques of communication are essential in leadership.

Chase's fourth standard involves the patience to get the facts. Often, emotion varies inversely with knowledge, and where prejudice is not deepseated the knowledge of the facts will change the judgment. One of the most poignant episodes in Mark Twain's *Huckleberry Finn* is used by Chase to illustrate the point. As Huck and Jim are floating downstream on the raft, Jim begins to talk about his little daughter, who had had scarlet fever, and tells how he yelled and cursed at her one day when she failed to close the door he asked her to close. Then he realized the truth "Just think, Huck", Jim says. "Deaf and dumb she was left by the illness, and me atreatin' her so." Knowledge of the facts serves a double purpose: it helps to prevent a person from taking action that later on he might regret; and it enables him to persuade others to a point of view that squares with conditions as they are known to exist.

Chase's fifth point is that individuals who are secure in their job relationships are happier, easier creatures with whom to work. Security seems to depend on a sense of belonging, of being wanted, on a feeling that one's contribution is important. Someone has said that it is hard to keep a chip on your shoulder when you are taking a bow. The aggression cycle often stems from personal insecurity and fear. Quite aside from the humane values of individual health and well-being, the toll of conflict will be enormously reduced, whatever the circumstances, when security can be increased.

PRINCIPLES FOR PROGRAMME ORGANIZATION AND OPERATION

A second broad area for the establishment of principles for administration is to be found in the executive function of programme organization and operation. Here, guides for action relate to the implementation of stated goals and objectives.

Interdepartmental Coordination

The Programme of a Department must be Coordinated with the Contributions of other Departments so that the Purposes of the Total Educational Programme can be Achieved

The attitude of the administrative head makes a considerable difference in the application of this principle. In some situations the nature of the relationships between a department and the total school is clearly recognized. Here the physical education programme is as much a part of the educational experience of students as any other phase of education, by reason of the excellence of the programme, interdepartmental coordination is a reality.

In other circumstances it may be observed that physical education is conducted definitely as an extracurricular experience. In these cases institutional policy accepts the separate status, and often dictates that it shall be separate. By relying on the gate receipts of sports teams for the financial support of the programme in physical education and athletics, administrative policy sometimes supports the separation of the department from the other educational aspects of the school programme. Only administrative leadership has the power to establish or to change a pattern or policy of this nature.

Department Objectives

The Main Purposes of Physical Education must be Promoted by Administrative Action

The physical education programme must implement the objectives which distinguish its contribution from that of other departments in total education. In addition to coordination with other departments, the unique purposes of its own objectives must be met. No other department is competent to do this and administration must provide the necessary leadership if the unique contribution is to be achieved.

Individual and Group Needs

The Needs of the Majority must be Served

The standard of the greatest good for the greatest number is operative here. And yet administrators must balance these considerations with recognition also of the minority group and the needs of specific individuals. These individuals need protection lest there be such dominance and control by the majority that their needs are ignored. The conflict of individual and group needs is often highlighted in the apportionment of facilities.

Facilities, or lack of them, are a particularly potent factor in the type of physical education programme which can be offered in any given school. Administrative action is the one over-arching influence which can implement the principle of serving the needs of the majority effectively. Specializations, vested interests, politics, small or large group influences all will be at work to promote particular interests and gain facilities for the practice of a particular activity. When facilities are inadequate and space at a premium, the resolution of conflict of various group interests is one of the most difficult tasks an administrators must face. He must find the delicate balance of providing for the needs of all within the limitations of available time and space and leadership personnel. Today's conflict situations may often be resolved through long-term planning. It is the responsibility of the administrator to see that inequities are recognized, and remedied with all due consideration to individual and group needs.

Equality of Opportunity

The Programme must be Organized and Operated to Provide Equality of Opportunity and Consideration for every Member of the Student Group

The implications of this principle are many. Individual differences will require the provision of activities suited to a wide range of individual skills and interests. Provision must be made for the needs of all groups: the handicapped, the beginner, the intermediate, the advanced, the highly skilled, and the expert. Equality of consideration will require recognition of each of these varied needs and interests of students.

Equality of opportunity will require a frank appraisal of many of the current practices where gross inequalities exist. Oberteuffer notes that in the budget of expenditures for one midwestern city the total expenditure for all forms of physical education for 290 boys was $47,326.77; the total expenditure for physical education of 120 girls was $35.65. The expenditure per girl was 29¢ and that per boy was $163.19. Actually, most of the boys fared quite as badly as the girls in this situation, for only those boys who were intermural athletes had any physical education activity. The argument that the boys programme was more costly because it involved interscholastic sports has no relevance in terms of the principle of equal opportunity for the values of the educational experience which was provided for the few. Sometimes the claim is made that the interscholastic programme must have the lion's share, since without it there would be no programme at all in that it supports the other parts of the programme. In this particular instance the facts of the case do not bear out such practice and it is safe to generalize that such support is seldom identifiable. If equality of opportunity is to be meaningful such administrative practices must be corrected. The administrative principle applicable here is discussed below.

Institutional Finance

All Aspects of the Programme should be Financed through the Educational Budget

The underlying premise here is the concept that any activity worthy to be included in the educational programme should be financed through institutional funds and that support from outside sources is not warranted. The need for seeking additional sources of revenue for the athletic budget, usually in the form of gate receipts from community support, as grown out of the influence of three factors.

The first factor is the concept that physical education and its laboratory experiences in the athletic programme is an extracurricular programme, a special service, a "frill". The second factor, directly related to the concept of physical education as extracurricular, is the rather common legislative restriction on the use of school monies drawn from the tax structure. The interpretation of the law in certain states has limited the use of tax money to the regular academic class programme. The third factor is the need for more money than the school can readily provide from its education budget. Physical education is expensive in comparison with certain other classes where laboratory facilities are not required. Modern practice demands a recognition and reconciliation of these factors in the light of the principles as stated.

3

The Definition of Educational Administration

With the possible exception of rate demands, few, if any, activities of local government have such a profound effect on the lives of most citizens as the education service and its administration. Few elements of local government are so little understood. All parents will be affected by the educational system and most will at some stage come into direct contact with their local education administration. Parents of young children may be dissatisfied with the provision for nursery and pre-school education and not infrequently such dissatisfaction may lead to parental organizations bringing pressure to bear on the administration. Once a child is of statutory school age parents become involved with the administration in securing a place in an acceptable school for their child, in obtaining grants of various kinds to assist them in providing adequately to enable the child to profit from his or her education, in obtaining school meals, in guidance towards a career and work, in the obtaining of professional qualifications for their children and themselves, and not least in securing recreative activities and continuing education for themselves.

The impact of educational administration on most members of the community is not only wide but deep. As the status of the United Kingdom has changed very rapidly from a wealthy world power to that of a highly developed industrial country competing to maintain the standard and quality of life of its citizens from its own resources, so a deeper awareness of the vital need to develop the skills and talents of young people to the full has spread throughout our society. The education service is seen as a most significant factor in national economic survival. Currently the perception is finding expression in the activities of bodies such as Universities, Polytechnics and the Training Commission and informs the vast legislative programme designed to achieve education for all children and adults which is of higher quality and more relevant to the demands of our increasingly complex technological society.

Parents are involved in increasing numbers in the management of institutions charged with the delivery of the improved quality of education.

If so many people are so acutely conscious of the importance of educational administration and the educational system which it provides, it is reasonable to ask why the nature of educational administration should be so little understood. There is probably no satisfactory single answer to the question, but it is the hope that the consideration of the nature of educational administration in the succeeding chapters will help to elucidate the problem. First it is necessary to look at the framework within which educational administration operates.

EDUCATIONAL ADMINISTRATION

It is significant that the first sections of the Educational Act, 1944 are concerned with the administration of education. No subsequent legislation has amended them. Part I of the Act is concerned with central administration and Section 1 provides as follows:

> It shall be the duty of the Secretary of the State for Education and Science to promote the education of the people of England and Wales and the progressive development of institutions devoted to that purpose, and to secure the effective execution by local authorities under his control and

direction of the national policy for providing a varied and comprehensive educational service in every area.

Part II of the Act is concerned with the statutory system of education, and deals first with local administration as follows:

[Section 6.2]
'The local administration of the statutory system of public education shall be conducted in accordance with the provision of Part II (of the First Schedule to the Act)' which provides that:

1. Every Local Education Authority shall, in accordance with arrangements approved by the Secretary of State, establish such education committees as they think it expedient to establish for the efficient discharge of their functions with respect to education and . . .
5. Every Local Education Committee of an LEA shall include persons of experience in education and persons acquainted with the educational conditions prevailing in the area for which the committee acts.

The authority for educational administration clearly establishes the central and local areas of the system and the interdependence of the two, although the position of central government as the senior partner is implied by the duty imposed on the Secretary of State to secure action by local authorities, and by the unequivocal responsibility to promote the education of the people. Subsequent variations of the detail of national policy have not affected the fundamental administrative provisions set out clearly in 1944. Before turning to consider the administrative functions of central government, it is appropriate here to mention the third statutory element of educational administration—the Chief Education Officer. Section 88 of the 1944 Education Act laid upon an LEA the duty of appointing a fit person to be the Chief Education Officer and after considerable debate during the period in which local government reorganisation was under review, this duty was retained by specific provision under the Local

Government Act, 1972. This statutory appointment (the only other office established by statute is that of Director of Social Services) at once gives the education service an appearance of uniformity and of difference from all other local government services, which has not always contributed to a full understanding of the public education system.

CENTRAL ADMINISTRATION

The duties of the Secretary of State are deceptively simple, but in practice are fraught with difficulties. Nowhere in the Education Act, 1944 or in subsequent legislation is the term 'education' defined. The Education Reform Act, 1988 goes some way towards definition by prescribing the requirements which must be satisfied by the curriculum of maintained schools. Since the curriculum is that which the school intends to teach, the requirements for the curriculum must broadly equate with what the school and the community regard as education. Those requirements are expressed in the 1988 Act as follows:

> The curriculum for a maintained school. . . is a balanced and broadly-based curriculum which
>
> (*a*) promotes the spiritual, moral, cultural, mental and physical development of the children at the school and of society; and
>
> (*b*) prepares such pupils for the opportunities, responsibilities and experiences of adult life.

Central government, through the Secretary of State for Education and Science, has extensive powers to prescribe elements of the curriculum, programmes of study, arrangements for assessing achievement, and to revise the National Curriculum as it is deemed necessary. Local authorities and governors are accountable to the Secretary of State who is advised and informed by various agencies such as HM Inspectors of Schools, the Curriculum and Assessment Councils, and such other bodies of enquiry as he may commission. To assist local authorities and governors in the task of delivering the curriculum he may issue instructions which have the force of law, circulars which are for guidance, research findings and special papers on specific aspects of curriculum. He has considerable power to develop particular areas of study, e.g. science, through financial arrangements and by controlling the supply and training of teachers.

The 1988 Act has sharpened the Secretary of State's powers and duty to promote the progressive development of educational institutions, e.g. by giving corporate status to Polytechnics and other Colleges of Higher Education, and by supporting the providers of City Technical Colleges. New administrative mechanisms are also brought into existence, e.g. the Polytechnics and Colleges Funding Council, all of whose members are appointed by the Secretary of State to support education and research in the Polytechnics and Colleges. City Technical Colleges are controlled by the agreement made between the Secretary of State and the promoters and by financial payments from the government. On the financial control of LEAs comment is made in a later chapter.

No less significant is the current accent on the importance of all pupils having some qualifications when they leave school. Here the Secretary of State is able to exercise considerable influence on the nature and content of education in schools by virtue of the fact that no course of study leading to an external qualification may be provided unless the qualification has been approved by the Secretary of State or by a body designated by him.

The Secretary of State appears therefore to have vast powers to enable him to fulfil the duties specified in the 1944 Act and amplified by subsequent legislation, notably the 1988 Act. Some dilemmas are already apparent. While for children in maintained schools a balanced curriculum is required, their contemporaries in City Technical Colleges are not offered a balanced curriculum but a broad curriculum with emphasis on science and technology. A consensus of opinion as to the responsibilities of adult life rarely exists and is of short duration. Within the space of less than fifty years the emphasis has shifted from physical fitness, to high technology, to skills required for industry, commerce and finance. Similarly the cultural patterns of society have changed during that period as have the predominant values of the adult population. At the same time individuals and voluntary bodies have through persistent and devoted work brought about changes in the attitude to children with special education needs which have found acceptance and embodiment in government policy.

Agreement on the purpose and nature of education is achievable in the broadest of terms. Acceptance of that agreement in a stable society rests on a basis of commonly held values, attitudes, cultural awareness and aspirations which are deeply felt but not readily definable. The paradox for the Secretary of State is that he must use precisely defined powers with sensitive, delicate and at times almost intuitive perception of the subtleties of essential shifts on that basis, if central administration is indeed to promote the education of the people and to secure effective execution of national education policy by local authorities.

LOCAL EDUCATION AND ADMINISTRATION

Local education administration may not be a flawless jewel but it is a thing many-faceted and of rare distinction. To avoid confusion it will be helpful to look separately at some of the main facets.

First it may be well to dispose of an issue on which much energy and time has been and will be spent—the almost metaphysical questions arising from the roles of the elected member and the Chief Education Officer. Where shall policy be made and where is the place of understanding is the sharp edge of the chisel with which critics seek to split the hard secure stone of local government. Occasionally members and officers tend to facilitate the cleavage by claims that policy is made exclusively by one or the other. Fortunately behavioural science has taught us that our assessment of our own role may be very different from the assessment of our role by another. Both have elements of validity and the reality of policy-making as distinct from the mechanics thereof seldom rests solely in one area. Moreover the Education Acts of 1986 and 1988 provide for the delegation of powers by the LEAs to governing bodies. Policy making in some areas is required by law to be a function of governors, e.g. whether sex education shall be given in the school, and if so, how. A further gloss on where policy is made is thus added, namely that policy as it affects the operation of a single institution may be made by its governing body. Local educational administration is therefore considered as the totality of all involved although inevitably much of this book will appear to reflect most strongly the viewpoint of the officer.

The most restrictive view of local educational administration is that which looks solely at the light reflected by the facet facing central government. Basically this view is that local government's function is simply to apply locally central government instructions. It is of course true that local government must operate within the limits prescribed by law and exercise only those powers which it is entitled by law to exercise. Powers exclusive to an individual LEA may be conferred by a Local Act or bye-laws made by an authority by viture of powers conferred by Parliament. Thus, for example, the bye-laws governing the employment of children may differ somewhat between one authority and its neighbours. But that in no way derogates from the principle that authorities must act within and fulfil their duties under the law. Indeed, in addition to the safeguards applying to all local government undertakings, the laws of education prescribe machinery for individuals to secure redress against unreasonable exercise of powers by LEAs and for the Secretary of State to enquire into any part of an authority's activities and to direct an authority to carry out a duty in case of default. Furthermore the 1988 Act provides for other bodies to assume powers to manage schools formerly maintained by the LEA while, at the same time laying on the authority a duty to carry out certain functions in respect of those schools.

The law not only imposes duties, but also confers powers. In many matters the authority is empowered to act if in its judgement it is beneficial so to do. For example, an authority may provide board and lodging otherwise than at boarding schools or colleges if it is satisfied that only by so doing can an individual receive suitable education.

THE NATURE OF EDUCATIONAL LAW

At first sight the law of education may appear quite precise. It is certainly voluminous. The Education Act, 1944 (which still remains the principal Act concerning the education system) has been amended or amplified by more than 20 subsequent Education Acts, including that of 1988, which is exceptionally detailed. Within that body of law are sections laying down the principles governing the provision and government of schools and the curriculum of primary and secondary schools, sections prescribing the provision for those with special educational needs, for school attendance, further education, medical inspection and treatment and finance. The rights of individuals, groups of individuals, parents, trustees and local government electors in respect of the educational service are set down and supplemented by other legislation, e.g. the Local Government Act, 1972, which defines the rights of the community to use school premises. The laws prescribe penalties for non-compliance with certain requirements, e.g. that parents shall cause their child to receive education either by attendance at school or elsewhere, and empowers the Secretary of State to make detailed regulations which have the sanction and force of law. It could well be supposed therefore that any ambiguities or imprecisions in the legislation have been cleared up or disposed of.

This is not so and the latitude of interpretation of the law remains wide. At the very core of legislation lies the fact that 'education' is nowhere defined. Such definitions as do exist are tautologous, *e.g.*:

> Primary education, that is to say, full-time education suitable to the requirements of junior pupils;
> Secondary education, that is to say, full-time education suitable to the requirements of senior pupils.

The 1988 Education Act goes some way towards definition by describing the curriculum of schools and laying down the core and foundation elements of the National Curriculum which are to form the major part of the curriculum to all schools. But even the core and foundation elements are qualified by the requirement that the knowledge, skills and understanding in each subject shall be attuned to the abilities and maturities of pupils. The duty imposed on LEAs therefore carries the responsibility of determining how and what educational provision shall be made in their areas, where decisions as to what shall be taught are made and how the needs of their areas are best understood and met. This is the great reality of educational administration demanding intelligence, vision, a lively appreciation of history, powers of analysis, synthesis and organization, but above all depth and catholicity of understanding of human condition and human aspirations. These are the qualities which the law implicitly requires of educational administrators although the one attribute specifically required is that of reasonableness.

A glance at the existing situation soon confirms that within the framework of law, powers are exercised individually by individual education authorities in the manner just described. When, in the reorganisation of local government in 1974, existing authorities were amalgamated into larger units considerable variety of practice between the constituent authorities was revealed. In some, children were transferred from primary to secondary schools at the age of 11, in others, children attending middle schools from age 8 or 9 years were transferred to secondary at 12 or 13, while the pattern of adult education varied from college-based to a diffused institutional pattern. As the former West Riding approached its end it published a paper which drew attention to the adequacy (or perhaps inadequacy) of the diverse provision made by some of the existing smaller authorities. Dramatically 1974 raised the curtain on educational administration and raised expectations that assimilation of authorities would lead to the adoption of the practices of the most enlightend. It also underlined the latitude which individual authorities have within the general framework of the law.

Changes in the law and in the application of the law affect the relationships between local education authorities and central government. The Secretary of State uses his powers to earmark expenditure to ensure that the development of certain aspects of education is accentuated. The 1988 Act gives the Secretary of State wide powers in many areas, notably in relation to the National Curriculum where he can establish and vary specific requirements. At the same time curriculum development work may be carried out at the instance of a local education authority with the Secretary of State's consent. Fears that financial constraints and inducements from bodies such as the training commission might unduly modify the curriculum at some stages of education have proved baseless. But the advent under the new legislation of institutions directly funded by central government yet part of the provision for the area will undoubtedly generate new situations for the administrators charged with the duty of providing a varied and comprehensive educational service for their area. Given the dedication of the Secretary of State to the promotion of the education of the people of England and Wales, and the provision of adequate resources, local administration has to use the whole framework of law to provide an economic, efficient, and effective educational system in its area.

REGULATIONS

It may be thought that the regulations made by the Secretary of State by viture of powers conferred by law would in fact prove to be a more prescriptive framework carefully defining the limits and nature of powers to be exercised by local authorities. To an extent this is so. The Schools Regulations for example lay down that 'in every school or department there shall be a head teacher'. It is not open to an authority, however reasonable it may appear, to organize schools wihout a head teacher. But two other prescriptions of the same regulations may be quoted as indicating the need for vigilance, adaptability and accommodation to change in educational administration.

> Classrooms shall not be overcrowded
> A pupil shall not be refused admission to or excluded from a school on other than reasonable grounds.

Given the needs of certain pupils and the methods desirable to meet those needs, a classroom which only 20 years ago was designed to house up to 40 children may reasonably be deemed capable of accommodating no more than 20. Educational administration must therefore constantly re-examine needs and practice to match resources to perceived requirements.

The second prescription illustrates the need to be aware of adjustments to the framework within which administration operates. What constitutes reasonable grounds for refusing admissions rests primarily with the local authority but on appeal the Secretary of State may and does on occasion reject the authority's view. Gradually, therefore, through case determination, practice establishes new known limits within which an authority may work. As no two cases are exactly similar the educational administrator must, being aware of practice and precedent judgement, determine how far such judgements limit the exercise of discretion in dealing with a particular case.

DEPARTMENTAL CIRCULARS, LETTERS AND GUIDANCE

Strictly speaking circulars, letters and other forms of guidance issued by the Department of Education and Science have not the force of law. Nor in the strictest sense are they statements of national policy. Despite the sometimes stenuous efforts exerted to persuade local authorities to comply with the guidance offered, it is nevertheless convenient to be able to withdraw such guidance quietly and unobtrusively. Thus while recognizing the genuine desire of central government to be helpful to local authorities called upon to deal with the unfamiliar as people from widely differing cultures become resident in this country, the convenience of being able to withdraw such advice by administrative process when events had demonstrated its unsuitability must not be overlooked. While, therefore, guidance in the several forms adopted by central government constitutes a less definable part of the framework of educational administration, it would be unwise for local administration to ignore such advice even though after due consideration of the circumstances it is decided not to follow the guidance offered.

CASE LAW

Practice reveals aspects of the law which are subject to a variety of interpretations, the final determination of the meaning of the law rests with the courts. After all the processes of appeal have been followed, the decision of the court is binding and compliance therewith obligatory. It is sufficient here to observe, that as the courts deal with specific cases, the law becomes clarified through judicial decisions and the educational administrator must be aware of the increasing definition of the framework in which he exercises the vast powers of interpretation alluded to above.

OTHER LEGISLATION

The many facets of local educational administration arise from the responsibilities which it must assume. The legal framework within which it operates is not merely that set by Education Acts. Certain powers, such as the power to employ staff, arise from the Local Government Acts and the position of the LEA as an employer means that it is subject to the law governing employment, protection of employment and insurance as is every other employer. In many authorities the direct responsibility arising from such legislation may fall on the Establishment or Personnel Committee, but no educational administrator relating to such diverse occupations as teaching, caretaking, building, engineering, secretarial work, technicians or school meals work, can afford to be ignorant of the provision of such legislation. The whole structure as well as the welfare of the staff or work force can by seriously affected by considerations arising out of employment legislation.

The Health and Safety at Work Act, 1974 bears even more directly on the person as well as on the work of educational administrator. Failure to comply with the provisions of the Act can be attributed to the individual responsible with the corresponding personal liability. But even more seriously the requirements of the Act can, it appears, operate so that the curriculum of an institution may be affected or even that certain activities in the institution have to cease. They must cause anxiety and concern for every educational administrator.

Legislation for the protection of the individual or of groups of citizens will continue to be enacted and in view of the wide range of educational activities will impact on educational administration. Two pieces of legislation deserve specific reference: the Sex Discrimination Act, 1975, which has already had some effect on the curriculum of schools, and the Race Relations Act, 1976. The latter is particularly significant for the way in which it permeates and requires positive action in every aspect of educational administration by requiring that local (education) authorities 'make appropriate arrangements with a view to securing that their various functions are carried out with due regard to the need. . .

> to promote equality of opportunity, and good relations between persons of different racial groups.

LIMITATIONS ON EDUCATIONAL ADMINISTRATION

Within the vast framework outlined the educational administrator is called upon to exercise powers with imaginative informed interpretation, but educational administration is subject to check. Of financial checks and audit more will be said later. Here it is necessary to refer to the safeguards against irrational use of power. The first and most far-reaching lies with the Secretary of State who can, if satisfied that an LEA has failed to discharge a duty under the Act, issue directions and secure their enforcement to ensure that the duty is carried out. This power has not yet needed to be exercised.

Any person may complain to the Secretary of State that an LEA has acted or is proposing to act unreasonably and if the Secretary of State is satisfied he may give directions to the LEA. This procedure has been invoked especially in connection with the placing of children in particular schools.

The Local Government Act, 1974 set up the Commission for Local Administration with Commissioners (Ombudsmen) with powers to investigate complaints of injustice in consequence of maladministration by or on behalf of a local authority. Increasingly the exercise of functions by LEAs has been restricted by successful challenges to specific action in the Courts, and by edicts from the EEC.

NEEDS OF THE POPULATION OF THE AREA

In considering the framework within which local educational administration occurs, it is necessary finally to refer to the duty laid upon LEAs to secure 'that efficient education throughout those stages (primary, secondary and further education) shall be available to meet the needs of the population of the area.'

The powers and duties of an LEA cover practically the whole span of human life. To meet the needs of the population implies an involvement in every level of human activity and endeavour. Even the apparently simple function of making adequate physical provision to enable the various stages of education to take place has been and is complex as later chapters will indicate but the task of ascertaining the spiritual, moral, mental and physical needs of the population is of enormous compass. Yet however vast and apparently beyond achievement the task may seem the educational administrator is from time to time called to account for his stewardship in this respect.

Investigations carried out by Committees of Enquiry and similar bodies have thrown light on good and indifferent practice in LEAs. Such investigations engender national and local debate which, at some point, almost invariably leads to a call for an appraisal of the contribution made by local educational administration. National perspectives also exert their influence on the provision looked for. Thus when there was grave concern arising from the rapid growth of sophisticated technology in certain nations, attention was focused on the ability of this country's educational system to produce men and women scientifically and technically equipped to generate an even more advanced technology here. More recently, when there was a widespread mood of depression and disillusion, the tendency to point to the failure of the educational system at all levels and to demand a reckoning of educational administration has been strong. Accountability for the operation of the education service is required—schools must declare their programmes and their success in achieving objectives (as measured by examinations); any person may be required to give or produce evidence to the Select Committee of the House of Commons and Her Majesty's Inspectors' reports are to be made public.

Alongside this 'market-place' attitude to the relationship of education to the community is to be set the impact of the media. On the one hand there is serious educational provision and information, e.g. Open University, Open Tech, numeracy and parental guidance programmes, and on the other entertainment and documentary feature programmes which often reinforce the image of education as a failure, at best irrelevant and wasteful and at worst harmful. The problems of anticipating, meeting and interpreting the needs of the population of the area are therefore an extremely important part of the framework of educational administration and will be a constant theme implicit or explicit throughout the chapters which follow.

How educational administration is, in fact, carried out and within the framework outlined is the theme of this book, and it is fitting that, in considering a service which is fundamentally concerned with people, we should first turn to look at the administrators themselves.

4

Policies and Programmes of Educational Administration

The most important consideration in administration is personnel. The members of an organization determine whether it will succeed or fail. The administrator must take into account the factors that promote cooperation, principles of good human relations, fallacy of final authority, importance of decisiveness, need for good staff morale, principles to be observed in personnel management, incentives for promoting cooperative effort, and the communicating process.

PRINCIPLES OF COOPERATION

The individual determines to what organization he or she wants to belong. The choice is conditioned by such motivating factors as purposes, desires, and impulses. After associating with an organization, services and relationships will depend upon how one is respected as an entity. The function of administration comes into force for reconciling conflicting interests, ideals, conditions, and positions.

Cooperation is essential to the successful functioning of an organization. Cooperation is effective and necessary to perform tasks that require a combination of human powers and to accomplish work that must be performed in a minimum amount of time. It is also important where the physical endurance and other human characteristics of one individual are insufficient—where group thinking is needed or where work must continue over an extended period of time.

To achieve cooperation implies that the specialties and unique abilities of individuals must be noted and utilized in situations where their services will be rendered under optimum conditions. The permanency of cooperation will depend upon the degree to which the purposes of the organization are achieved and individual motives are satisfied. The function of the executive is to see that these essentials are accomplished.

THE INDIVIDUAL AS A MEMBER OF AN ORGANIZATION

How may individuals be expected to react as members of an organization? This is a question that should be asked by all interested in administration.

An individual may act in many ways, depending upon his biological make-up. Action can be impulsive and unpremeditated, caused by certain drives or impulses. A response may be one of fear, anger, or joy. The action can be habitual, the result of learned acts performed under select conditions. It may be rational, a result of having several alternatives to follow; under this circumstance, action is taken only after consideration of the various issues involved. Or action may be intuitional, based on a feeling that some specific action should be taken, because of instinctive perception rather than careful logical thought and reasoning.

Each individual is different and is made up of a combination of characteristics. The action that he takes will depend upon what he thinks will contribute most to the establishment of the ego.

Each individual wants to be recognized, have a feeling of belonging, and maximize his ego. The process that determines whether such goals are realized is social in nature. Everyone recognizes that group action is essential to the establishment of self. Therefore, membership in organizations is sought. Whether or not one is accepted depends upon what one has to offer in the way of service or specialized abilities. An organization's recognition of an individual's contributions results in satisfaction and self-esteem. The building of self or the development of ego can occur in all types of associated activity, whether it be at work, home, school, church, or in some other setting.

The associated efforts involved in the work experience of the individual should be satisfying. This is where most individuals spend a considerable amount of time. If the individual is not recognized, cannot grow and develop, does not feel that he belongs, he will look to other areas for these essential human needs. In so doing he may neglect his work and even become obtrusive in his efforts which, as a result, may affect many other persons. An organization's success depends upon each individual member's being an essential and important component of the total process.

The administrator in the capacity of leader must recognize the importance of each individual in the organization. Leaders who are trusted and friendly, who recognize importance of group goals, and who have respect and concern for each member of the group will motivate behaviour which is happy and productive.

Every administrator should seek to imbue the organization with the theme that every individual has a stake in the enterprise. The enterprise can be successful only as all contribute to the maximum of their potential. With the success of the enterprise will come increased satisfaction to each individual. Above all, it must be recognized that submergence of self is necessary for the achievement of the organization's goals.

THE FALLACY OF FINAL AUTHORITY

The administrator is often envisioned as an executive who occupies a very high position with absolute power. He can hire and fire at will, he can issue orders covering a wide range of areas, and everyone in the organization is subject to his every whim and desire. He is looked upon as having the supreme and final authority over all his subordinates and their every act. The administrator is seen as a "Scrooge" who gives orders to various "Bob Cratchets."

This idea of administration has come down through history from the ancient kings who possessed absolute authority over their subjects and from men in high positions who seized or inherited great power. Such powerful individuals still exist today in some of the Fascist and totalitarian states of the world. However, in this country where democratic principles pervade such authority is a fallacy.

Final authority in any one individual's hands is a dangerous weapon and should be permitted only in rare instances. As one author has stated, "Administrators hold power and where humans hold power there is temptation to tyranny; and where there is temptation, there is yielding." Francis Bacon said, "The one who has power thinks he can command the end, yet rarely has he patience to endure the means." Whitehead concurred when he stated, "The enjoyment of power is fatal to the subtleties of life." Prince Kropotkin is more direct in his answer when he says, "It is a commonplace of history that power is poisonous to those who exercise it."

Modern-day administrators must rely on the other members of their organizations for the achievement of their objectives. Decisions are reached only after several members, all of whom have interests bearing on the judgment, have deliberated. Many of the decisions are made by individuals who are subordinate to the administrator at the top. Plans are worked out, reports are made, and the spade-work is often done by the lower echelons, leaving only a routine approval by the man or woman at the helm.

If the administrator takes the sole authority for making decision without consulting others, many judgements will be wrong because of lack of information. Organizations function best when informed thinking is brought into play. President Eisenhower, upon taking office, pointed out that he was depending upon his various Cabinet members and other government officials to make many decisions, leaving only the most important issues for him to decide.

The authority that does exist belongs to the job and not to the person. The administrator should never feel powerful and all-important. Authority does not reside in one human being but in the best thinking, judgment, and imagination that the organization can command. Every individual has the authority which goes with his position and only that much. In turn this authority is conditioned by other members whose work is closely allied to his in achieving the objectives for which the organization exists. Authority comes from those who perform the more technical aspects of the organization's work as well as from those who, because of their positions, are responsible for the ultimate decisions. Department heads, foremen, and staff consultants issue reports interpreting the facts. Their judgments, conclusions, and recommendations contribute to formulation of the final decisions that are the responsibility of the administrator. If these interpretations, judgments, conclusions, and recommendations are not accepted, the organization may fail. Its best thinking has been ignored. Furthermore, individuals cannot be induced to contribute their efforts in an organization that has little respect for their thinking. Authority is not resident in one person. Instead, it permeates the entire organization from top to bottom.

Naturally, there has to be compliance by the members of the organization with orders that are handed down by administrators. This is essential for the efficient running of any organization. Most individuals will comply with such orders, provided they understand the communication, it is consistent with the purpose for which the organization exists, is compatible with their interests and incentives as members of the organization, and they are capable of complying. Administrators must keep these facts in mind in issuing communications. Sometimes it becomes necessary to issue orders which do not conform with the individual's wishes. In such cases there must be good reason for such action. In addition there should be some preliminary explanation and persuasion or an offer of inducements in order that the issue will be overlooked. Everything should be done to avoid denial of authority.

At times when there is flouting and disregard of authority, it becomes necessary to sever an individual's association with the organization. Attacking an organization or intentionally disregarding assigned duties should result in punitive action, even to the point of separation from service. Rules and regulations that exist grow out of practice and are made in the best interests of the organization. They help in the achievement of objectives. They must be adhered to.

STAFF MORALE

There are certain definite conditions which are known to contribute to staff morale. Some of the more important of these will be discussed. Administrators should continually strive to create such conditions in their organizations. The degree of good staff morale that exists will be in direct proportion to the degree to which such conditions are satisfied.

Leadership

It goes without saying that the quality of the leaders will determine staff morale to a great degree. From the top down, there should be careful selection of all individuals who act in leadership capacities. Other things being equal, individuals will contribute better service, produce more, have an over-all better morale, and have more respect for individuals who are leaders in the true sense of the word. This is also important from the standpoint of attracting the most outstanding persons to an organization. Human beings do more than brick and mortar and other material things to induce the best minds and the most qualified persons to join an organization.

There must be mutual trust and confidence between leaders and other personnel. This is essential for obtaining the moral support that is so necessary to the establishment of good faith on the part of all. Furthermore, only as this good faith is established will the operating procedures be carried out in the most efficient and effective way possible.

Physical and Social Environment

Good physical and social environments are essential to good staff morale. The health of the worker must be provided for. There must be good lighting to protect the eyes, good air to protect the lungs, and adequate safety precautions to protect the body. There must be provisions for mental health which include proper supervision, provision for advancement, provision for any emergency that may arise, and provision for intellectual improvement. Anything that is conducive to physical, mental, and emotional health is important to the morale of the individual and in turn to his efficiency as a member of the organization.

The social environment is also an important consideration. The individuals with whom one works and the activities in which one engages can strengthen or dampen the spirit. An individual is the product of his interactions with others. Therefore, in order to improve oneself it is very important to associate with those who can contribute to this improvement. Since the working day represents, to a great degree, the majority of an individual's social relationships, it is important that these relationships be wholesome and conducive to individual improvement.

Advancement

Human beings like to feel that they are "getting ahead in the world." This is an important consideration in developing and continuing a high degree of staff morale. This consideration necessitates informing each member of an organization as to what is essential for progress. Opportunities should be provided for self-improvement in learning new skills, gaining new knowledge, and having new experiences. In addition, encouragement should be given those who are anxious to improve and are willing to devote extra time and effort for such a purpose.

Performance records should be available so that personnel can determine the degree to which they are achieving their goals, their weaknesses and strengths, and the requirements necessary for promotion. A broad programme of in-service training should be established in every organization to provide adequately for this essential requisite to staff morale.

Recognition of Meritorious Service

Another requirement, similar to advancement, which is a requisite for staff morale, is recognition for outstanding contribution. As has been previously pointed out, all human beings have an ego which likes to be flattered. Those who make outstanding contributions to the organization should be recognized. This is very important to further greater achievements.

There should be provisions for material awards in the form of salary. This is one incentive that is used in American society as an indication of accomplishment. Therefore, in order to have good morale and also to compete with other organizations, this is necessary. There should also be provision for other incentives, such as position with additional prestige, commendation, and public acknowledgement. It is essential to acknowledge the progress that an organization is making and the contributions of the members who make such progress possible.

PERSONNEL MANAGEMENT

There are certain principles that must be recognized in dealing with personnel. Every executive must understand such truths if he or she would administer wisely.

Level of Performance

It must be recognized that, over a long period of time, the level of performance of individual members of an organization will be determined by the performance of the individual who occupies the highest executive position. Individuals who are competent cannot seem to produce at their highest level for an extended period of time if they are encumbered by weak leadership. The leader sets the pace. An organization, to function at its highest efficiency, must have at the top a person who is also "tops" in efficiency. It is a fallacy to think that a weak leader can be surrounded with outstanding associates and produce great results. In time the poor leadership will reflect itself from the top to the bottom of the organization.

Selection and Dismissal of Personnel

The manner in which the administrator selects, keeps, and dismisses personnel will determine to a great degree his success as an executive.

Only the most competent individuals must be selected. The individuals who have proved themselves in their jobs should be retained. The administrator's ability to provide incentives and to use the power of persuasion will determine whether or not key personnel are kept. Finally, the way in which an administrator deals with incompetent and obtrusive individuals will determine in great measure the state of morale and efficiency of the staff.

Identifying the "Individual"

Every individual member of an organization wants to be a member of the team and feel that he is making a recognized contribution to the group effort. This implies that he wants to know what is going on, how his contribution is aiding in making progress, and that he belongs.

The administrator must recognize that the human being is the "end" and not the "means to an end." His or her job should provide for release of creative human talents in an associated enterprise. This demands the conception of personnel not as workers turning out a product or rendering a service for a master but as a collection of individuals who are partners in the endeavour. Through such an approach there will be established a loyalty to group effort which will increase services and make production "hum."

Respect for the human personality must be the main consideration in all administrative action. The human element is the most valuable factor in all life. Hundreds of man-hours are utilized in the search for one person lost at sea. Untold wealth is spent to free a coal miner trapped in the ground. Similarly, in an organization, attention must be focused on the human being. The goals that are set in terms of inanimate things must first be evaluated in terms of the animate. Technology must give way to what is best for the human being. All policy and practice must reflect an emphasis on the individual in personal relations.

Obtaining Confidence of the Staff

In order to win the cooperation of their staffs, administrators must be cognizant of several requisites.

Administrators must win the confidence of their staffs. Regardless of the reputations they have when they take the posts, their success in being accepted and gaining the trust of their personnel will depend on what is done after they take over the "reins of authority."

To win the confidence and cooperation of staff members requires that administrators be honest and sincere. When they are wrong they should admit their errors. At times they must divulge unpleasant truths. They must never be sarcastic. To be insincere with an associate will result in loss of confidence. Individuals recognize that administrators are not perfect, but at the same time they expect an admission of error when it exists and a conscious and sincere desire to understand problems.

Administrators will gain the confidence of the members of their organizations only as their actions unfold from day to day on the job. They are the masters of their own destinies.

Welfare of Personnel

Administrators and organizations should recognize that in personnel management the welfare of the individual must be provided for. There must be adequate medical protection, pensions, recreation facilities, safety precautions, sickness benefits, and accident compensation. In addition, as has been pointed out, there must be good working conditions in respect to light, air, temperature, and sanitary conditions.

A point that is very important, however, in making provisions for the welfare of employees, is that good human relations cannot be purchased. Good working conditions are essential to human welfare but cannot be used as a substitute for the principles of cooperative effort and human relations that have been previously discussed. They are details that should be attended to in the name of human decency and in order to provide the most favourable setting for productive effort. The administrator cannot take the attitude that "Now that I have given you all these things, I can order you around any way I would like and disregard good human relations as much as I wish."

The Money Motive

Those who deal with individuals must realize that money is not the only thing that motivates human beings. They cannot have the attitude that, since they have provided a large salary, they do not need to provide any further incentive.

Any administrator who makes such an assumption is due for a big disappointment. An organization cannot exist on a purely economic motive. It is a factor that should be considered, but it is limited in its potentials. Individuals want something more than money out of a job. An actual experience points this up. One individual in a school position was given a thousand-dollar raise one year. The chairman of his department continually referred to the raise as the solution to any and all problems that existed in regard to this person. However, there were many other factors in regard to that individual's welfare which the thousand dollars could not solve. In fact he moved to another position the following year.

In addition to money, individuals want recognition, prestige, a faith in the leadership provided, and the knowledge that they are contributing to a worthy cause, are making others happy, and enriching their lives through their endeavours. In this day and age when so much stress is placed on material things, it is very important for administrators to recognize that a good raise and a large salary are not panaceas for every problem.

Individual Differences

An important principle of personnel management is the recognition of individual differences and different types of work. Individuals differ in many ways—abilities, skills, training, physical, mental, and social qualities. There are also various types of work which require different skills, abilities, and training.

These differences in individuals and types of work must be recognized by the administrator. One of his or her main duties in respect to personnel should be to make sure that the right person is in the right niche. An individual who is a "round peg in a square hole" does not contribute to his own or to the organization's welfare. To be placed in a position which should be held by a person with lesser qualifications or vice versa is unjust and devastating in its results.

It is important for the administrator to recognize in some formal way individual differences that exist in the organization. A system of status must exist for purposes of communication and orderly procedure. Such system of status must be readily understood, authoritative, and authentic. These systems of status not only make for better communication but also provide the basis for personnel improvement and advancement within the organization. Furthermore, they help to develop a sense of responsibility in the individual. The status that is granted to any one person should be in line with capacities and importance of the function. Many disruptive features can develop in status systems if there is no recognition of individual abilities, if the system is allowed to become an end rather than a means to an end, and if proper incentives are not provided at each level.

COMMANDMENTS FOR ADMINISTRATORS

Henry has discussed eight commandments for administrators which should be read by every person who is interested in furthering good personnel relations. In substance these commandments are as follows:

1. The administrator who gets the best results is the one who is deeply interested in people.
2. The administrator should not take any administrative action until he has consulted with those individuals who are likely to be affected.
3. The administrator should be able to laugh at himself.
4. The administrator should never criticize an employee before his colleagues.
5. The administrator, to be effective, must lead the way and not just give the orders.
6. The administrator is interested in passing on to his colleagues everything concerning his job that they are able to learn.

7. The administrator should classify all information as to whether it is secret and should remain in confidence or whether it can be passed on. Passing on secret information is being disloyal to colleagues.
8. The administrator recognizes that employees want more than money out of a job. Such factors as recognition, respect, and loyalty are the extra pay desired by every human being. The good administrator is one "who pays (employees) a little each day from his soul."

INCENTIVES AND PERSUASION

Individuals contribute services or produce goods because of certain motivating factors. These motivating factors can be called incentives. Energies are expended and efforts put forth because of incentives. Since individuals are the most important factor in an organization, it is very important that incentives be considered.

Newman points out various incentives, on which there is considerable agreement in management, to which most human beings respond.

1. Higher financial income
2. Social status and respect
3. Security
4. Attractive work
5. Opportunity for development
6. Worth-while activity
7. Personal power and influence
8. Treatment of each subordinate as an individual person
9. Voice in his own affairs for each man
10. Just and diligent supervision.

Man is motivated as certain incentives are brought into play, or on the other hand, as certain bad features of work are decreased. For example, if one's salary is increased, it acts as an added incentive whereas if excessive working hours are decreased, that also acts as an incentive. There is also another consideration in viewing incentives. The individual's state of mind is very important. A person's attitude will determine whether certain incentives can act as motivating factors. This consideration is very important in the field of religion and education where the desire to render a service and the desire to do good are attitudes of mind which motivate action.

Types of Incentives

There are many types of incentives which result in an individual's associating with an organization and thence contributing his energies to its success. Some of the more outstanding incentives are discussed below:

1. *Material Items.*— Some of the most attractive incentives in this day of interpreting values in terms of material possessions are such items as money and shelter. These serve as incentives for most people up to the subsistence level. However, beyond this point, most individuals need additional inducements.

2. *Non-material Items.*—Such incentives as prestige in one's work, a position where one's power is felt, or where an individual is tabbed with the title of "man or woman of distinction" are very important to many people. Individuals will sometimes forego high salaries and other material possessions to gain these non-material things.

3. *Optimum Physical Conditions.*—It is important to most persons to work in an atmosphere and setting where there are good physical conditions, such as light, heat, and fresh air in the immediate surroundings of one's endeavours. In addition, the general geographical section of the country plays a major part. Some desire a warm climate all year. Others like the mountains and still others like dry air. These represent incentives which motivate persons to select certain locations.

4. *Satisfaction of Personal Ambitions to Do Good.*— Individuals are frequently spurred on by personal desires to do good. The desire to serve one's family and one's neighbours, the desire to render a service to one's community, the desire to satisfy personal ideals, and the desire to produce a thing of beauty which will provide aesthetic satisfaction to many—these are incentives which are very important in the lives of many individuals.

5. *Belonging to an Attractive Organization.*—Some individuals like to be associated with a recognized and well-known organization, or one that has certain features attractive to them personally. This may mean being on the faculty of an "Ivy League" College, associated with the National Broadcasting System, the Riverside Church in New York City, or Twentieth Century-Fox Studios. These are well-known institutions, and, for some, to be identified with an organization that is known is an incentive. Others find certain organizations attractive because of the persons or employees who work there. Attraction might be based on such conditions as freedom from racial hostility, a place for professional growth, or means of satisfying personal ambitions.

6. *A Harmonious Pattern of Work.*—Persons like to associate themselves with an organization where methods of work are familiar, attitudes are similar, and practices are known. Through years of experience the individual becomes set in his ways and in his thinking. He desires to associate himself with organizations that think and work along similar lines—ones which he knows and likes.

7. *Mental Health.*— Individuals prefer working conditions which are conducive to good mental health. Many desire such things as freedom from tensions and conflict, absence of highly competitive working conditions, security on the job, and absence of strain. They do not want to be tied down to their jobs to such an extent that these interfere with their family and community responsibilities. Many are willing to accept less pay and chance for advancement in order to have these conditions.

Persuasion

In many cases it is necessary for an organization to change the thinking of individuals so that the incentives which it has to offer will be attractive. This may be called persuasion. All administrators should possess the art of persuasion if they would surround themselves with the most competent individuals.

Men's and women's minds may be changed by coercion or by education. Some individuals join organizations because they have been coerced into joining. Slaves in pre-Civil War days were forced to work on certain plantations. Young men are drafted into the Army. Labourers are many times denied certain benefits unless they join the union. These are examples of coercion. Individuals are forced to cooperate. All will recognize that this type of persuasion is not the type that is most productive of goods and services.

Some individuals join organizations because they are persuaded that it is in their own interest and welfare to become a member and cooperate. People usually do not contribute and become members unless they are convinced it is worthwhile. Through education, it is possible to persuade individuals of the need for cooperating with certain organizations. The area of religion provides a good example of the individual's being educated from the time that he is very young, through adulthood. Through religious instruction and indoctrination the person develops a need for joining a particular church. Thus the individual has been persuaded through education to "belong." The art of persuasion can also be accomplished through an appeal to patriotism or the idea of service to a worthy cause.

The important item to remember when providing incentives is that all individuals cannot be treated alike. The administrator must recognize that different individuals are motivated by different incentives. What moves one person to action will not necessarily move another. Another point is that administrators are unable to offer all the incentives that are needed to get the cooperation that is necessary. Therefore, the thinking of some individuals must be changed through the art of the administrator's persuasion. Through a combination of incentives and persuasion the most competent individuals can be brought into an organization, where as members they will contribute the cooperation that is needed for successful accomplishment of purposes. Some incentives are necessary—some persuasion is also necessary. Through a balance of both, progress will be made.

COMMUNICATION AND PERSONNEL RELATIONS

Communication has been previously referred to as the lines of authority within the structure of a formal organization. A system of communication is essential in order to have an efficiently run organization. The system should be clearly understood by all personnel so that conflict will not ensue. This is essential to good personnel relations. The following are some important rules to keep in mind in regard to the system of communication.

Channels of Communication should be known by all Members of the Organization

Through the use of organization charts, education, announcements, and other devices, the administrator should leave no doubt in anyone's mind as to each person's position in the system of communication. Official appointments should be made known, each individual should understand the nature and scope of his position, and the lines of authority should be definitely established.

The Importance of a Formal Line of Communication

All members of the organization should understand why it is important that every person be responsible to some one individual and why such formal relationship is necessary to efficiency. The administrator should explain these things to his staff if they are not already clearly understood. Individuals will cooperate more readily if they understand the need for such organization.

The Line of Communication should be as direct as possible

There will be less opportunity for misunderstanding if the line of communication is short and direct. Communications are given either orally or in writing and the greater the number of coordinating centres through which they have to pass, the greater is the chance for error. There is also the danger of a misinterpretation as the communication progresses through many individuals. The administrator should recognize this principle and, in setting up or revising the structure of the organization, should provide for only as many positions as are absolutely necessary for purposes of communication and coordination. If the administrative organization becomes too large, it becomes cumbersome, bureaucracy develops, red-tape ensues, and the efficiency of the organization breaks down. The lines of communication should be clear, logical, short, direct, and within the understanding of all.

The Line of Communication should be used, once it is established

With few exceptions, communications should pass through each coordinating centre of the formal line of authority. Administrators should know what is going on. This is possible only if communications pass through them on the way up and on the way down. In addition to the importance of keeping key persons informed of various actions, this is also important from the standpoints of eliminating conflicting communications, having proper interpretation as the communication progresses through various levels, maintaining responsibility, and insuring that the prestige of executives is maintained. These important considerations will not be possible unless the system of communication is observed from top to bottom.

Under certain circumstances, individuals in the lower ranks of organization have business to transact directly with individuals in the higher echelons of authority. To provide for such a condition, there should be some provision for direct lines of communication to the top.

Competent Individuals must occupy the Positions of Authority

In order to ensure a high degree of morale, efficiency of operation, and effective cooperation, it is essential that only competent persons occupy the positions of authority in the formal line of communication. Good communication exists only where there is respect, confidence, and trust in those individuals who have been assigned key positions.

Emergencies must be provided for in the Communication System

When a key individual in an organization dies, when a chairman of a department is unexpectedly absent from work, or when some other emergency occurs, the lines of authority must continue to operate. An organization survives and accomplishes its objectives only if it has provided for continuous operation at all times. This is similar to the adage known in the theatre: "The show must go on." Regardless of what may happen, the play must go on as scheduled. Similarly, in any organization, regardless of the nature of the emergency, provision must be made so that the responsibilities are fulfilled. One can readily imagine what would happen if the President of the United States were killed and there were no provision for a successor. It would make the country weak and vulnerable. The same thing could happen to any organization.

All Communications should be valid and authentic

Communications will be accepted only as they are authentic and valid. This means that the individual who issues the communication has authority to assume such a responsibility and that it is an official communication. The administrator should be careful not to exceed the authority and responsibilities of his office. This is essential to a recognition of and faith in any system of communication.

SUPERVISION

The supervisor is a key person in the promotion of good personnel relations within an organization. Administrators should be very careful to select and utilize in supervisory positions only those persons who will be most effective in developing the highest type of associated effort.

Within a school setting, for example, Wiles points out, "Supervision must provide: leadership that develops a unified school program and enriches the environment for all teachers; the type of emotional atmosphere in which all are accepted and feel that they belong; opportunities to think and work together effectively as a faculty group; personnel procedures that give the teacher confidence in the school system; and program change based on honest evaluation . . . skill in leadership; skill in human relations; skill in group process; skill in personnel administration; skill in evaluation."

Supervisors can be helped to do an effective job if they follow the personnel policies that have been listed in this chapter.

An example of what is being done in the Long Beach, California, Public Schools to provide effective supervision in the area of physical education is listed below. These in-service teacher education techniques are now being used by physical education supervisors:

1. The first interview with the applicant for a position in physical education gives the supervisor an opportunity to establish standards expected of all physical education teachers.
2. The traditional staff breakfast held on Saturday preceding the opening of school in the fall does much to acquaint teachers with other personnel, build group morale, and give teachers a feeling of "belonging."
3. Group meetings are held with new teachers prior to the opening of school and early in their first semester to acquaint them with the Long Beach schools, explain courses of study, and get them familiar with the over-all policies in physical education. A plan of frequent visitation during the first months of service to give any assistance needed is also followed.
4. The self-rating form developed in the physical education office serves as an excellent means of acquainting teachers with sound methods in physical education teaching. It also assists principals in judging the efficiency of physical education teaching.
5. Group workshops are conducted on specific techniques for specified grade level groups, either mixed or separated by sexes—depending on the content to be considered.
6. Group workshops are carried on for specific subjects, such as orthopedics, modified physical education, gymnastics, coeducational activities, et cetera.
7. Local teachers are often used in the planning and subject presentation at meetings and workshops. Senior high

school and city college teachers are often used in demonstrating sport skill techniques for junior high school teachers. Any teacher with recognized good teaching skills may be used when appropriate. This technique helps much in tying the programme together for all grade levels.

8. Demonstration teaching is done at intervals by physical education supervisors.
9. The bringing in of recognized specialists in various fields, as speakers and panel or workshop leaders, has proved successful.
10. Physical education class demonstrations conducted for parents in the various schools have been very successful and profitable. This technique is encouraged and assisted by the central office supervisors and helps develop good teaching techniques as well as give parents a better concept of the broad physical education programme.
11. The physical education office always invites the participation of teachers in the formulation of courses of study, physical education policies, planning of facilities, selection of institutional supplies, and many other special projects.
12. Participation in the regular staff meetings in the various schools gives supervisors an opportunity to assist in many specific problems.
13. The Gym and Field publication put out bi-monthly by the central physical education office serves to bring good philosophy, new programme ideas, new publications, and other valuable information to teachers.
14. School visitations as requested by principals and/or teachers give many opportunities for supervisors to assist with programmes, content, and methods.
15. Teacher requests for supervisory assistance get a prompt response.
16. Self-initiated visitations to schools are made in the interest of helpfulness rather than inspection.
17. Letters and verbal expressions to teachers in appreciation of teaching and other performances well done and/or noticeable improvements are techniques

used by all physical education supervisors when such techniques are justified and appropriate.

18. Some inter-visitation and observation within our own school system has been done by teachers in the past. When well organized and done with definite objectives it is an excellent technique for in-service education.
19. All physical education teachers are encouraged to join appropriate professional organizations, attend conferences of such organizations, and subscribe to professional publications.
20. Teacher attendance is encouraged at institutes of general nature in education fields closely related to health, physical education, and recreation.

'ips" for On-the-Job Effectiveness

1. Take a positive and friendly approach, looking for something good being done.
2. Take an interest in the welfare of the teacher and his family—new members of family, new home, vacation plans, et cetera.
3. If some phase of the programme is not going too well ask, "Have you ever tried this?"
4. Give responsibility for some phase of work and give all credit due when the job is carried out. People "arise to the occasion" when called upon and growth takes place. Especially good for hesitant people.
5. If the teacher has a problem, analyze it with him and make clear suggestions or, if there is some research to be done, do it at an early date and report what you have done.
6. Be fair, honest, frank, and consistent.
7. Be quick to give recognition to all jobs well done.
8. Be tolerant, patient, tactful, and calm and exhibit trust and faith in the individual. Initiative and enthusiasm are contagious.
9. When requests come for assistance respond to them quickly. It is today the help is needed, not a month from today.
10. Inform immediate supervisors of good work you have noted.

11. Activities or programmes that are planned by all are usually made effective by all.
12. "How do you think we could improve this?" is always a good approach.
13. Always keep channels of communication between teacher and supervisor open at all times.
14. Keep informed on what is going on in all schools.
15. Use local people, doing good work, in workshops, demonstrations, et cetera.
16. Work for the teachers' welfare at all times.
17. There are many ways of "finding" your way into places where there may be a way you can help.
18. Get well acquainted with all people with whom you work. If you know and understand a person well, you will certainly know better the proper approach.
19. Fundamentally teachers want to do the right thing. Approaching them with this attitude is helpful to both the teacher and the supervisor.
20. Encourage the expression of ideas by all. If presented in a group note the response of others.
21. Try to put yourself in the position of the teacher. What would you expect of a supervisor if you were the teacher?
22. Seek information: "How do you do this at your school?" This type of question helps the teacher to analyze his own method and often encourages him to improve.
23. The supervisor can achieve teacher confidence by doing an efficient and helpful job.
24. Encourage people with a common interest to work together.
25. Do everything possible to eliminate the feeling of the teachers that you are coming to "inspect" but radiate every evidence that you are coming to encourage and help.

5

What is Democratic Educational Administration?

Democratic administration is essential if the American way of life is to continue and become a permanent feature of this culture. It is of especial importance during this day and age when freedom is being challenged from all sides, when men cannot work and fight for their beliefs without fear of investigation, when guilt by association is commonplace, and when education is under fire.

EDUCATION AND GROUP PROCESS

Education is frequently under attack. Schools are often accused of not teaching the three R's, of allowing subversives to infiltrate the ranks of teachers, being Godless, using discipline that is too rigid or too lax, and conducting experiences where not enough facts are mastered. Probably those who claim that educators are not democratic are more justified in their attack than many others.

Although education is moving more and more along democratic lines, there is still ample evidence that democratic procedures are not widespread. The consumer of the product does not have much to say as to what he should be taught; boards of education prevent certain textbooks from being used in the classroom; many teachers are barred because of race, colour, or religious faith; the problems of segregation have not been finally settled; and some administrators rule autocratically.

Public school education in the United States is deeply rooted in democratic principles. The schools should be a place where democracy flourishes. School is a place to learn, make mistakes, experience social control, develop initiative, and become creative and productive. Schools should teach individuals how to develop responsibility and self-reliance, and to understand their fellow-men. Authoritarian practices prevent such development and education. President Griswold of Yale University defines democracy as " . . . a political society in which the greatest possible measure of justice implicit in the phrase 'equal opportunity' is combined with the greatest possible measure of freedom and encouragement for the individual to develop his own talent, initiative, and moral responsibility." This is a goal for all educators.

Administrators must recognize and believe in these democratic essentials in order to direct organizations in a manner which can be truly labelled "democratic." They must have greater knowledge of the learning process, of such things as how learning takes place, the effects of coercion, the importance of sympathetic guidance and social interaction, individual differences, and desirable goals. Autocratic administrators will determine the policies, make the decisions, and literally "run the show." If administrators go to the other extreme and believe in a *laissez-faire* or "hands off" policy, they do not furnish the necessary guidance and leadership which is their responsibility. Instead of following either of these two extreme approaches, they should try to give that type of democratic leadership which provides for participating as a member of the group and arriving at policies and decisions through group thinking rather than unilaterally.

Democratic administrators must have good human relationships. They must have faith in people and in their ability to do constructive thinking. They must understand human beings in order to recognize those who do and those who do not contribute to group goals. They must be able to motivate all to communicate and participate. Furthermore, they must help in the in-service training of staff so that they, too, will critically evaluate scientific evidence and personal opinion.

The administrator should recognize certain steps in the democratic process of a staff and organization working together in order to accomplish group goals. Some of the steps that should be considered are as follows:

1. Goals should be developed through the group process. The goals that are set should be attainable, challenging, and adapted to the capacities of the members.
2. Good morale should be developed among the entire staff. This is an essential to constructive group action. A permissive climate must be established in group deliberations. All must feel a sense of belonging and recognize their important contribution in the undertaking. A feeling of "oneness" should pervade the entire group.
3. Group planning must be done in a clearly defined manner. A stated procedure should be followed. It should be a cooperative undertaking, based upon known needs and flexible enough to allow for unforeseen developments. The fulfilment of plans should bring satisfaction and a feeling of success to all who participated in their formulation and accomplishment. All should share in recognition for a completed job.
4. In staff meetings and other group discussions the administrator must encourage utilization of democratic principles. Each member's contribution must be encouraged and respected. Differences of opinion must be on a "principle" basis rather than on a "personal" basis. The organization's objectives and purposes must be continually kept in mind. All members must be encouraged to facilitate the group process by accepting responsibility, alleviating conflict, making contributions, respecting the opinions of others, abiding by the will of the majority, and promoting good group morale.
5. There must be periodical evaluation of progress. The group should evaluate itself from time to time as to its accomplishments, in terms of the organization's goals and the effectiveness of the group process. Each individual must

evaluate his own role as a member of the organization in respect to contributions made to the group process and the accomplishments of the group.

PROBLEMS ASSOCIATED WITH THE DEMOCRATIC PROCESS

Application of the democratic process to the functioning of an organization does not solve all problems. Instead, many situations and difficulties arise because of elements that are inherent in the application of democratic principles. It is important to recognize these problems and cope with them as they arise. Despite such dilemmas, the advantages of the democratic process far outweigh the disadvantages.

The Problem of Divided Opinion

In a democratic organization, it is assumed that the wishes of the majority prevail. There is a question that often arises in this connection: Is the majority always right? Very often an important issue will be determined by one vote. Students of history remember that during post-Civil War days Andrew Johnson failed by one vote to be found guilty. Every individual can recall similar situations within organizations where like results have occurred. Is this a weakness of democracy? Should important problems, plans, and issues be decided by such a small difference of opinion?

It seems that the reasoning behind such a dilemma is clear. All who believe in democracy recognize the importance of having as much unanimity of thinking as possible. However, they also recognize that it is much better to have a majority make a decision than to have it made by one person who is an autocrat.

Also in this connection, there is the problem that individuals who have opposed an issue must conform to the will of the majority, if democracy is to exist. The solution is very clear. A democracy requires cooperative action on the part of all. Unless this follows, democracy deteriorates. There are numerous incidents familiar to all when opposing groups have failed to comply. Many who voted against the Eighteenth

Amendment to the Constitution refused to comply. In the area of athletics many of the schools that were in the minority and voted against the so-called "sanity code" and other curbs on "big time" athletics would not conform and broke the rules. This cannot happen if democratic principles are to work. A functioning democratic organization or society depends upon compliance with the will of the majority. Only in this way can it survive.

The Problem of Subjective Personal Opinion as Opposed to Scientific Fact

In many democratic discussions it appears to some individuals that scientific evidence should dictate policies, and personal opinions must not become involved. On complicated issues situations develop where certain individuals are acquainted with scientific data which in themselves define the issue. Therefore, the conclusion is reached that discussion, voting, or other devices are useless since the course of action is very clear as indicated by known fact.

The answer to such a problem seems to be that there will be acceptance if individuals know and recognize the facts. Generally acceptance fails to materialize when evidence is not conclusive or when it has not been properly publicized. The democratic process can contribute immeasurably to such enlightenment. Through discussion, facts can be presented and understanding reached. Individuals with reasonable intelligence will accept scientific fact as against personal opinion, if the presentation is clear and the evidence is convincing. William Gerard Hamilton during the late eighteenth century made a statement which has a bearing on this point. "Two things are always to be observed; whether what is said is true in itself, or being so, is applicable. In general, things are partly true, and partly not; in part applicable, and in part not. You are careful therefore to distinguish; and to show how far this is true and applies, and how far not." The democratic process is the most effective method yet devised to show what is true and applies.

The Problem of Standards

A question that is often raised in connection with the utilization of the democratic process is: What does it do to standards of performance? There is a belief in some quarters that by allowing majority opinion and decisions to prevail, standards of performance are lowered to a "middle level." The individuals who have a low set of standards tend to pull down those with high standards. In effect, this results in a compromise on middle ground. The standards take on mediocrity rather than remain at a high level.

The answer to this problem is difficult. A democracy rests upon the worth of the individual. It has faith in the individual, in the goals that he will set, and the standards he wants to follow. The challenge presents itself to those whose standards are high to bring the rest up to their level, rather than to allow themselves to be relegated to a lower one. Such a process may take time. Results are not always immediate in a democracy. Nevertheless, the principles upon which it is based are sound. By utilizing such principles as freedom of discussion and assemblage, it is possible to educate and to elevate standards.

The Problem of Time

Democratic discussion with their need for deliberation and agreement take time. Such delay often creates problems, sometimes with serious consequences. There is often too much delay between the need for action, decision, and execution. Democracy is based upon the necessity for individuals to see the need for a course of action and then, after seeing this need, deliberate it, and finally see that the decision which they have made is put into effect.

It is true that this dilemma often works to the disadvantage of many individuals. However, it does not necessarily have to be this way. It has been seen how rapidly the Federal Government will act in case of emergency. For example, it did not take long for Congress to declare war after the attack on Pearl Harbor, or to vote the necessary supplies and help once our country was at war. The delay occurs when there is misunderstanding, a situation is not meaningful, and the course of action is confusing. Perhaps it is wise in many cases to have this lag of time. Hasty action also results in many mistakes.

The element of time is usually important in cases of emergency. Democratic organizations make provisions for action under such conditions. Members of an organization can vest such powers in qualified individuals when necessary. John Locke in his *Treatise on Civil Government* pointed out that sometimes it is inevitable that decisions be made quickly by the executive in charge. It would seem logical that the wise administrator and organization would provide for such emergency action.

The Problem of Discussion with Uninterested and Non-informed Individuals

Another problem which frequently arises in democratic deliberations is that some individuals who participate in group discussions are many times not interested or competent to discuss intelligently and constructively the subject at hand. Such a situation may be very helpful as an educational device. As individuals become better informed on various topics they contribute more. Many minds are better than one or two. Any group should welcome as much help as possible in solving problems.

The Problem of Authority

Criticism has often been directed against the democratic process from the standpoint that it results in confusion and poor direction. The authority for certain acts is not clearly established. Furthermore, it is conducive to a conflict of ideas, which results in indecisiveness.

It seems important to recognize the part that democratic principles play in such a problem. A democratic organization vests in its members the right to help determine policies, purpose, and methods. They want a "say" in these important factors which vitally affect their lives. At the same time, however, they vest authority for execution of policy and purpose in administrators who are responsible to the group for their actions. Any democratically run organization has to recognize clearly the definite lines that exist between policy forming and execution. If an individual has been placed in an administrative position, the wherewithal to perform duties effectively must also be granted. In a sense, all individuals have authority in their respective positions. Authority goes with the job and not with the individual. This is true from the top to the bottom of the organization. There is no "final authority" except as it exists in the entire membership. All organizations that are to be efficient and effective must clearly recognize these principles upon which the functioning of an organization rests.

The Future of Democracy

The problems that have been listed should not be used to deter the application of democratic principles to any organization. If one takes any other method of government, it would readily be found that problems of much greater magnitude and seriousness exist. Furthermore, the administrator as a leader can do much toward solving and alleviating the difficulties that are associated with democratic dilemmas. Outstanding leadership is essential to any democratic organization. High-quality leadership will stress the importance of group participation, freedom of action, good human relations, and the importance of each individual member. This is important and far outweighs any advantages associated with systems that are not democratic.

It can readily be seen that a great amount of responsibility falls upon the shoulders of the administrators. The desire, technical knowledge, drive, and other qualifications which often come to mind first should not disillusion one into thinking that it is possible to be a good administrator without the knowledge or intent of utilizing democratic principles. The administrator's success in the long run will rest upon his ability to lead a democratically organized and functioning organization.

6

Educational Planning and Administration

Planning is the fundamental activity of educational administration in all its various aspects and at all levels of operation. To fulfil their legal obligation of effectively executing the national policy for providing a varied and comprehensive educational service in their area, Local Education Authorities must create an efficient organization. Careful planning is the instrument by which such an organization can be created. Nothing in life is static and no organization is sufficient for all time. The continuing need to plan in an education service arises because things change continually. In order, therefore, to understand the planning processes in educational administration, it is first of all necessary to look at the dynamics of the system—the major sources and causes of change.

THE DYNAMICS OF THE SYSTEM

Four major categories of pressure for change or adaptation in the education system can be identified: political; professional; demographic; and changes in related services.

Political Initiatives

Education law places with the Secretary of State the responsibility to promote the education of the people of England and Wales and the progressive development of institutions devoted to that purpose, and to secure the effective execution by local authorities, under his control and direction, of the national policy for providing a varied and comprehensive educational service in very area. These words prescribe very succinctly vast and complex responsibilities. The exposition of those responsibilities in the 1944 Act probably represented the closest approach to political consensus on the aims and scope of the educational service which the country has experienced in the last 50 years. It was generally accepted therefore, that although education is administered locally and, as will be seen, large policy initiatives have been taken by LEAs, the many aspects of the service are now settled by Westminster and Whitehall.

Major political initiatives have been taken since 1944 by central government; for example, reorganization programmes to eliminate all-age schools, legislation to enable the establishment of middle schools, the introduction of comprehensive secondary education, bringing the most mentally handicapped children within the scope of the education service, the development of higher education in the public sector and its later removal in large parts, the virtual disestablishment of mono-technic teacher training institutions, and the raising of the minimum school-leaving age on two occasions. All such initiatives require considerable planning for their implementation by local authorities.

In more recent times, governments have become much more interventionist, most notably in the shape of the 1988 Education Act. The national curriculum and testing, arrangements for substantial delegation of powers to governing bodies in schools and colleges and proposals for open enrolment have re-emphasised the sometimes latent power of the centre to take major initiatives. Indeed the nature of the 1988 Act lays much emphasis on the LEA's planning role. Whilst detailed administration is devolved to individual schools the LEA is expected to concentrate on strategic planning issues, such as monitoring and delivery of the national curriculum, and overall plans for the delivery of work-related non-advanced further education. In addition, an armoury of specific grants such as those for In-service Teacher Training and Education Support have appeared. Often funded by siphoning off part of the education element of the block rate support grant, these have provided central government with a much more direct leverage on educational developments at local level. But the local authority will continue to have an important role in planning the delivery of such schemes. Specific grants are no longer confined to DES; the Department of Employment, the Training Commission, the Department of the Environment and the Department of Trade and Industry have also become active in this field. As examples 2 and 3 at the end of this chapter demonstrate, the development of bids to central government based on detailed and far-reaching plans has become a very important task for education departments.

Within an LEA itself political initiatives may arise from the education committee or the council, from governing bodies of schools and colleges or from voluntary bodies such as the churches, parent-teacher associations or specific pressure groups. Whatever their source, they become policy when they have been considered and approved by the authority. Examples of local initiatives in which the principle involved is so urgent as to require its adoption regardless of all other consequences are extremely rare. Generally speaking therefore any such initiatives should be examined carefully and thoroughly planned before the policy decision is taken. The planning process will include consideration of all the factors—including resources—necessary to the implementation of the policy arising from the original initiative.

It is perhaps, in this respect that the two kinds of 'political' initiative most importantly differ from the point of view of the Education Officer of the LEA. Any new policy or adaptation of existing policy approved by the authority itself ought, by definition, to have understanding and support for its implementation among the reievant professional and political groupings in the authority's area. The planning for the change takes place within a framework of known resources, well understood objectives and an agreed time scale. Consultation prior to the decision merges into planning groups and working parties subsequent to the decision. Representatives of those responsible for the implementation of policy are likely to have been aware of the initiative from its inception (and frequently party to its promotion). The planning required is therefore likely to be advanced through existing structures and to be well within the capacity of those involved. Feedback from those introducing the change is likely to be relatively easy to achieve. School reorganisations and local curriculum initiatives belong in this category.

By contrast, initiatives taken by central government, even if they have been the subject of consultation with local authority associations, are unavoidably more remote from the officers, members and teachers of the LEA. Sometimes they are politically unwelcome to the majority group on the council. Nonetheless, if they are a legitimate fiat of central government their introduction has to be planned by the LEA. The details of the planning processes are considered in a later chapter. The necessity to use senior staff time and skill, to ensure adequate memoranda and explanation to the committee, to lay bare resource implications and to set forth the limits of LEA discretion within the proposed national policy all do however require emphasis here. The planning processes set up in consequence of national initiatives frequently need to be specifically created for their purpose; to include members as well as officers from an early stage; to ensure considerable consultation with teacher and the public; and involve the necessity to reach agreement with treasurer, architect, planners and others within the authority about resource implications. The development of formulae for financial delegation to schools and colleges as required by the 1988 Education Act provides a prime example. So too do the preparations for the introduction of competitive tendering in the areas of school meals, cleaning and grounds maintenance now required by legislation. The process of planning in response to central government initiatives is not essentially different from that involved in responding to local initiatives, but it is often longer, more demanding of senior officers' time, and more complex. This is because central initiatives cannot reflect the variety of local circumstances. Moreover, in responding to a central political imperative such as parental choice as expressed in open enrolment policies or the opportunity for schools to opt out of local education authorities altogether, such initiatives can, by their very nature, make efficient planning at local level very difficult indeed.

Of course, political initiatives, whether of central or local government, do not arise out of thin air. They emerge from the existing state of the service and the climate of opinion in 'the political nation'. This climate is partly created by the other three parts of the dynamics of the system, which we must now consider.

Professional Initiatives

The 'profession of education' is properly wider than many professions. Central to the service are professionals such as teachers, advisers, administrators and academics. Less directly or exclusively involved are workers in allied fields of human science and behaviour, such as philosophers, economists, political scientists, sociologists, paediatricians and psychologists whose work nevertheless can have a direct bearing on the objectives and methods of the education service. Those concerned with educational provision have therefore to be sensitive to contemporary research and practice both in pedagogy and in other related professional fields which influence the contemporary view of human nature and what the state should attempt to offer its citizens.

Professional initiatives affecting the education officer may arise from, for example, national or local curriculum developments or research, the teachers' associations, HMIs, advisers and administrators. DES requirements to issue a major statement on the whole curriculum, policy statements on the place of science or modern languages, curriculum development initiatives, such as the project on economic awareness and oracy and education support grant activities such as rural schools or information technology, all require LEA planning. But these are only a few of the outstanding manifestations of the constant search for more appropriate, and surer ways of educating all the children within our schools. The search by well-informed, highly dedicated and energetic people is almost limitless is range and variety. It is part of the professional expertise of the educational administrator to be aware, as extensively as possible, of this incessant quest for improvement. More important, he must be equipped to distinguish the most promising among many possible innovations, know how current practices may be modified to benefit from such innovations, understand what, from the past, needs to be jettisoned and through channels such as training courses, reports to committees and brief to architects, ensure that new approaches are thoroughly understood and beneficially applied. Increasingly he needs to know how to shape and prepare plans which will be acceptable to those at the centre of responsibility for allocating specific funds.

Demographic Change

The dynamic caused by population changes is always with us. Any account of the education service since 1944 very soon involves describing how 5 million school pupils in 1947 became nearly 10 million in 1972 (including the raising of the school leaving age first to 15 and then to 16); how 207,000 teachers were employed in schools in 1950 compared with 404,000 in 1974; and how the population of England and Wales shifted internally from old urban areas to new suburbs and new towns so that to the problems of providing for growth were added those of providing for redistribution.

Population growth was the general theme until the mid-seventies. Since then, however, a major trough in numbers has developed, passing through the system to reach the upper end of secondary schools in the early 90s. It is not a symmetrical trough. Current births and future forecasts do not promise as return to the peak numbers of the past. Superimposed on these national patterns are local variations, sometimes very marked, together with a wide range of future forecasts. Such a complex and changing situation means that educational planning at LEA level needs to be constantly reviewed and monitored.

Other Services and Cooperative Action

One of the most striking features in the field of social provision since the last war has been attempts to bring about cooperation between discrete services. The intellectual origins of these attempts lie in focusing upon the client or client group rather than upon the service organized predominantly around a single professional discipline. Consideration of the needs of the young child and his family, for example, transcends the confines of any one discipline. Doctors, health visitors, teachers, and social workers may all be involved in the welfare of the child and family. And once inter-disciplinary thinking has been accepted inter-disciplinary working becomes an imperative.

Of course much had already been done within the limits of individual authorities. An excellent example is the close co-operation between the pre- and post-natal health services, the hospitals and the education services to provide a diagnostic and supportive service to handicapped children and their parents. The tremendous advances in the education of deaf children owed much to this cooperation. Intermediate treatment depends for much of its success upon cooperation between social services and education; whilst cooperation between education and the police service and the initiatives taken by the Training Commission over the Youth Training Scheme and, most recently the Employment Training Scheme for older unemployed require a considerable response from the further education service. Such developments represent the acceptable face of corporate (that is, cooperative) planning in local government and allied services. They demand in the educational planner a wider vision and secure professional roots.

THE CONSTRAINTS UPON PLANNING

The greatest constraint upon educational planning is the inevitability of starting from where you are. Virtue in educational planning consists partly in acquiring and making use of a profound understanding of the existing system and partly in accepting realistically that most change, however carefully planned, will be gradual and unspectacular. This should not obscure the fact that from time to time the various dynamics already mentioned lead to a situation where planning and planned change must be so urgent and immediate that their effects are sudden and disturbing. The restructuring of teacher training to match the falling school populations or measures to deal with youth unemployment are examples which come readily to mind. Nevertheless it is true that plans should never be based on any starting point other than present realities. They should provide for the evolution of the existing system so that it has some new, desired capacity. For this reason it seems likely that 'the planning function' in an education service should never be too far divorced from the experience and understanding which comes from taking responsibility for day-to-day administration. The 'thinkers' and the 'doers' should not be allowed to drift far apart from each other. Five different kinds of constraint, or rigidity, in the existing system may be analyzed.

Existing Policies

The authority will probably already have a policy upon the matter which the planner is about to tackle. It may be a policy to have no policy; or it may be a policy which needs changing; but in either case it will have collected around itself a set of public expectations, political implications and assumptions in the clerical and administrative staff which together constitute a formidable inertia. These factors need consideration early in the planning process, for they exercise a powerful influence on the preparation, presentation and implementation of plans. Minorities or an ill-informed administration can substantially frustrate change earnestly desired by the majority.

Existing Procedures

The explicit or implied policies which have just been mentioned will be enshrined in clerical and administrative procedures ingrained in the staff of the authority. The power of procedures—whether written or conventional—should never be under-estimated. It is of vital importance to the administrator, therefore, that staff, at all levels, should be adequately trained and alert to the need constantly to ensure that procedures are the most efficient instruments for effecting policies and that they do not degenerate into rigid constrictions of desirable improvements.

Existing Staff

Neither should the impact upon staff, whether clerical, manual, administrative or teaching, of asking them to change their ways be underestimated. Planning, which is an instrument for improving a service for people should always provide for the human elements, although there is an understandable tendency for the concrete issue of providing buildings, equipment and transport to assume an undue prominence.

The education authorities of this country have experienced over the last 45 years an unprecedented amount of change. Curricula, school and college organization, teaching methods and forms of administration and political authority have all been radically realigned. As we seek evidence of the effectiveness of much that has been attempted, the importance of understanding how the 'critical unit of work' really works (the teacher in his classroom, the head with his staff, and adviser in his team, the education officer in his hierarchy, the committee in their divided world of care for the service and fear for the rates) is being driven home to us more and more. Where things seem to have gone wrong, there is often to be found at the root a failure really to understand what the innovation was for and to make a commitment to it and feel a new sense of motivation. This is especially a danger when the planning has been prompted by external, unwelcome forces for change. Where it has had to be 'reactive' rather than 'proactive'. Perhaps worst of all have been the half-understood innovations which have led to good ideas being introduced in a superficial way and with lack of rigour so that they become discredited. Educational planners must face these traumata of their psychological past and yet must avoid feeling too scared to take any bold decisions. Instead they should provide in the future more sensitively for preparation and training of those who have to make new systems work.

Existing Buildings

The procrustean bed is never more starkly revealed than when the existing stock of buildings seem inappropriate for its future use. Fifteen per cent of the country's primary schools still date from before 1903; many secondary schools are on split sites; colleges of further education are working in annexes and makeshift accommodation. The qualitative problems are, however, greater than those of quantity. The 'open school' is hard to achieve in a railway carriage of classroom compartments; integration of departmental effort in a college of further education is difficult to achieve when departments are spread over several sites. The planner must judge what it is reasonable to expect the staff to achieve against the odds: get it right and you raise people above themselves; miscalculate, and you destroy morale.

Finance and Budget Forecasts

The planning process requires some realistic estimate of the future flow of resources into the sector of the services under consideration. This is often the most difficult of all the variables to assess. Buildings, number of staff, their state of training, the theoretical objectives, can all be researched and known fairly accurately. This is especially the case when local government finance is manipulated by central government for purposes of national economic management. For an individual LEA the more significant factor in finance planning is often the rate support grant, not local views about service levels or willingness to pay the rates. Locally expenditure is generally determined for one year only and this one year at a time. The politically-fraught revenue budget of the local authority system is inimical to good planning. The creation of a five-year forecast budget, rolled forward each year looks fine in theory but presents far too many hostages to fortune in practice for it to have been widely attempted. Whilst the financing of local government is now to be reformed, it is unlikely to present the educational planner with a much firmer basis for his work. With the community charge contributing a much smaller percentage of their income to most authorities than rates, their dependence on finance outside their direct control will become even greater.

The Planning Process

We can now see what good educational planning ought to involve. It should mean deriving from the dynamics of the system things which either should be attempted or which those in power are determined to attempt (the two are often the same thing) and proposing workable ways of doing them, in the light of the constraints.

Logically, four stages can be seen. In the real world, of course, they often turn up in a different order or occur simultaneously in different parts of the authority's deliberative processes—so that the planner has the additional task of bringing some order to the process and keeping the appropriate groups and individuals in touch.

Choice and First Thoughts

At any one time a Senior Education Officer is probably aware of a dozen potential and pressing initiatives which would meet some or all of the criteria set: they would gain political support; changes in demography or teaching methods make them desirable; they could be achieved within existing or likely future resources. Increasingly they are influenced by central legislation. But it would not be possible to sustain so many initiatives simultaneously. There appears therefore to be a need for a kind of standing policy review process. It does not always require the formality of a sub-committee of the education committee; yet it is essential that there is some member involvement. In practice, in most authorities, it is the Chief Education Officer and the chairman reflecting together and exchanging ideas and information from their two overlapping worlds who carry out this review process. It is reinforced by the general network of relationships between officers and members, especially between heads of branches and sub-committee chairmen. The chairman may be backed up by regular meetings of all members of the controlling group at which policy is discussed. Where there is a 'hung' council all or most political groups will be involved. Equally the Chief Education Officer has various policy planning and review groups which maintain the health of the professional network through their contacts with advisers, schools, academics, HMIs and the literature. Both are regularly stimulated, indeed often nettled, by a flow of advice and criticism from practitioners and the public.

From this continual (and often half-incidental) review of the existing state of affairs, there emerges a manageable flow of ideas or projects which merit working up into discussable form because they appear to meet needs that are real in ways that would gain professional and political support. At this stage they are written up by the appropriate education officer as discussion documents, or consultative papers or draft committee memoranda.

To make this over-rationalised picture real, it is necessary to add that much important policy-making is done against the clock, because, say, a new specific grant is announced or curtailed by some central government department at short notice, or because a legal case or ombudsman report requires urgent consequential action. Most likely of all, it will be because of last minute changes in budget provision. In such cases chairmen and education officers must rely on their experience in coming to a decision and the process of 'getting the feel' of the political and professional climate has to come at later stages when first drafts may need radical revision.

Political Decisions about Policy and Resources

When preliminary consultation and redrafting have finished, the policy proposal gets its first exposure to the formal consideration of an education sub-committee. That may lead either to a crisp decision, if the subject matter makes it possible, or to a more formal series of consultations with interested groups—especially teachers, governors and parents. Each of these will require from the education officer careful timetabling, preparation and recording, eventually leading to a further comprehensive report to the committee.

Increasingly the education officer will need to think about policy at two levels, that of the LEA and that of the governors and individual schools. As much greater delegation to schools becomes a feature, the ways in which a central LEA policy will be shaped and interpreted at school level will also be of considerable significance and there will certainly be interaction between the two levels.

Professional Decisions about Methods

Once the policy makers have decided the outlines and objectives of the new policy, the professional is faced by the need to choose the optimum method for bringing it into the authority's practice. Again, a sharp, clinical distinction between 'professional' and 'political' cannot be made. At the extremes there is no difficulty: the Chief Education Officer can assume that he is free to decide how to administer policy for the employment of part-time assistants in school kitchens. At the other end of the spectrum, the method by which existing schools are converted into a tertiary system, for instance are as much part of the public-political decision pattern as is the principle of comprehensive education itself. Between extremes, issues which would appear to rest entirely within the jurisdiction of the Chief Education Officer may because of topical interest become socially or politically charged and implementation of policy then requires a more open exposition.

Agreement about a Plan

The final stage is the agreement among those whose assent is required. With the greatly increased central powers conferred by the 1988 Act on the Secretary of State, this may mean the holder of that office. In this case preliminary soundings will have been made with DES. It may require a committee report, whose preparation will involve consultation with teachers, other Council departments and any other interested parties. At a lower level, it may simply require a clear memorandum to all concerned in which the plan and any consequential administrative measures are explained.

At this point the necessity to write clear administrative and clerical instructions and train staff in their application becomes paramount.

Feed-back

All planning, to be realistic, needs feed-back from current experience of attempts to implement plans. And any particular policy needs to have, built-in, a servo-mechanism by which its application is refined in the light of experience.

To achieve this it is essential that the educational administrator should always be firmly in touch with daily practice whilst retaining, amid the mass of detail, clarity of vision, insight and imagination.

The structure of the LEA administration should be created with this need as one of the criteria. The complexity of the modern education office is itself considerable; add the necessary connections with teacher-groups, other staff-groups, voluntary bodies and with other local government departments or extra-local government services and the need for good management becomes obvious. Later chapters will analyze key planning tasks of the LEA in more detail. But perhaps a few examples chosen from the fields, cooperation with other local services, curriculum development and response to a national initiative will helpfully complete this 'overview'.

EXAMPLES

1. A Joint Venture—Education, Health, Social and Voluntary Services

The Children's House and Playpark' in a northern industrial town was built by the LEA under an urban aid programme and involves education, health and social services in its functioning. The direction of planning was undertaken in the education department and illustrates all the main dimensions.

In the late 1960s the Council had made a survey of day care facilities for the under-fives and declared its belief that, wherever possible, health, education and social services should be coordinated and should emphasize also the contribution of voluntary organizations and especially participation by parents themselves.

When the opportunity of an urban aid project appeared there was added to these objectives that of providing safe, open and imaginative play space on the model which had impressed a recent Council visitation to Scandinavia.

The project was, therefore, complex and novel. It involved finding a suitable site in a declining urban area; pooling the ideas of three statutory agencies; learning about adventure playparks; surveying the voluntary groups of the chosen area to see how far present needs were being met; working closely with the building and landscape architects; and maintaining a tight cost-control system. At a later stage, as the scheme emerged from the discussions and sketch plans, consideration of appropriate staffing, management and administration had to be solved. Finally, the decision was taken to let the venture develop slowly and free from publicity so that the first two or three years of operation also became part of the planning process with much important development of the use of the buildings being done through the process of experience.

Following the initial approval of the concept, site and cost limits by the committee, a project team under the leadership of the Assistant Education Officer for Primary Education was created consisting of education advisers, playing field officers, project architect, head of the adjoining primary school, the District Education Officer and the local parks officer, social services and health representatives and representatives of the various local voluntary organizations associated with the pre-school child and the family. From a series of fairly unstructured meetings there emerged the elements of a possible scheme which was then worked up into an architect's brief and interior finishing and design brief.

Local neighbourhood support was essential to the success of the scheme; not everyone would necessarily welcome a children's playpark adjacent to their home and the existing play groups or mother and toddler groups might feel threatened if they thought the statutory services were merely moving in with well-resourced alternatives to their existing efforts. Steps were taken, mainly through the existing primary school, to work with and through parents of young children in the area. The site was designed to add a visual asset to the area; the use of the building would not be a conventional nursery school but more of a 'drop in' centre where families could develop their own efforts with the help but not the dominance of professional teachers. It would also be a place where they could meet representatives of the local health and social services without a special journey and in relaxed circumstances which made it more possible to understand their purpose and value. Most of all, the Children's House would try to help young parents as they faced the problems and joys of bringing up their young children.

By the end of two years the building and playpark were ready and a small permanent staff, already known to parents in the area, and the local primary school staff, appointed. The furniture had been selected to add colour and texture. Floor coverings, cushions, curtains and easy chairs absorbed noise and gave an air of home. Parents and young children found it easy to enter and work in the various rooms and spaces. Their relationships with the staff were direct and on more equal terms than is common in school, office or clinic. The local health visitor found her contact with mothers and very young children especially easier.

But this was still in the planning stage. The first summer holiday's operation of the playpark taught a great deal; the community began to reveal new capacities which required new styles of organisation. The decision to avoid publicity and visitors paid off: all those working at the centre concentrated on the job in hand without the self-consciousness that questions posed by visitors might have aroused. The senior advisers of the authority kept in close touch and ensured that the adjustments of furniture, operation or relationship with 'the office' that became necessary were deftly achieved. The planning process probably lasted at least two years after commissioning the building, as well as the two years beforehand.

2. *Planning the Delivery of WRNAFE (Work Related Non-advanced Further Education)*

Throughout the 1980s the delivery of vocational further education has been subject to close scrutiny from a variety of bodies, including the DES, Audit Commission, TC and local authorities. Particular attention has been focused on the efficiency of the delivery by reference to such indicators as staff-student ratios but recently attention has also focused on the effectiveness of delivery, i.e., are objectives being met.

This movement to a more rigorous assessment of the performance of further education providers has, of necessity, led to consideration of the planning mechanisms of the delivery of further education. The MSC in particular have required LEAs to produce an annual development plan for NAFE. In this particular case study we see how the local authority moved from ad hoc arrangements to a more systematic and structured approach which directly relates the planning process to the allocation of resources.

When the MSC (now the Training Commission) announced in 1984 that LEAs would be required to produce an annual NAFE development plan, the local authority found that it did not have the staffing resources or systems in place to tackle the production of the plan in other than an ad hoc way. Statistical informatior was requested from the authority's colleges and was collated and drawn into a draft plan by a degree student on placement from a local polytechnic. The draft plan was then edited by a senior officer. Information was not collected in a structured way. Lines of thought on important development issues were not clarified before the information was requested. Colleges did not identify with the plan or accept any ownership of it. When finalized, the document was not so much a plan as a series of general and position statements which, in themselves, did not require action nor did they put forward a strategy or clear objectives.

It became clear to all concerned that a radical change was necessary if the plan was to achieve its objectives of ensuring that course provision reflected the needs of the local labour market, that courses were provided efficiently and effectively, and that development needs were identified and solutions proposed.

Therefore, the format was changed so that

(*a*) The document was a plan of intended action (not a position statement) setting clear objectives against which performance could be assessed.

(*b*) The document established mechanisms to ensure that the objectives stated were automatically considered as part of the Council's budget process.
(*c*) The plan established systems to ensure that it was regularly reviewed and performance evaluated.

A secondment was arranged with the MSC whereby an experienced member of their regional NAFE planning team was based in the Education Department and under direction from the Assistant Director (Further Education) took responsibility for producing as a discussion document a first draft of a three-year plan. A NAFE Planning Group comprising Principals of Colleges, the MSC Further Education Officer, the Assistant Director FE and the seconded officer was established.

In view of the experience gained, the team recommended that a Planning Group be established on a permanent basis with the membership as above but with the addition of the College Industrial Liaison Officer, the Authority's Planning Officer and the LEA Adviser for staff development, all of whom had a significant input into the production of the plan.

The group established an annual planning cycle, as outlined overleaf, which was designed to produce the plan in a structured, coherent manner and also incorporate the Authority's response to the joint efficiency study on managing colleges efficiently. The Authority's response to the issues identified in the report was to strengthen planning procedures generally, to plan and monitor course provision and projected student numbers, and to allocate resources to colleges, not on the basis of historical budgets but by reference primarily to full-time equivalent student numbers. As the WRNAFE plan established projected FTE student numbers its conclusions fed automatically into the allocation of resources to colleges. At the same time the Authority introduced new management controls which allowed college managements the opportunity to benefit from the planning process. Virement and net budgeting in particular were introduced.

The impact of the changes is yet to be assessed in detail but will be considerable. The strategic role of the LEA will be enhanced as it will now be provided with comprehensive reports upon which it can establish priorities and assess performance.

College management are aware that planning documents now determine resource allocations and, as a consequence, specific plans have to be established for marketing, staff development and curriculum provision. These must relate to the overall WRNAFE plan.

It is intended to monitor closely the effect of these changes, particularly on the demands of senior management and to consider what, if any, changes are required to reflect the new approach.

The table on next page shows, in summary form, the overlapping processes involved as between WRNAFE planning with the Training Commission (column 1), the College's total course provision planning arrangements (column 2), and consequential budget adjustments (column 3).

3. Management of Specific Grant-aided Provision: LEA Training Grants Scheme (LEATGS)

In promoting its policies for education during the 1980s, the Government instituted specific grant funding for a number of programmes managed by LEAs. In all such schemes, funding is subject to the acceptance by the funding agency of detailed LEA proposals, normally related to indicative expenditure allocations or other spending targets. The LEA Training Grants Scheme is one such scheme and provides grant aid at the 70 per cent rate in national priority areas of training and 50 per cent in support of locally determined needs.

Limited specific grant aid for in-service training of teachers was introduced in 1983-84 in support of training in national priority areas. That scheme was further extended in the years that followed. The 1986 Education Act established the LEA Training Grants Scheme by abolishing the teacher training pool and giving the Secretary of State new powers in respect of the funding of in-service training for teachers and other groups. The process by which one LEA implemented the scheme gives an example of the planning and management processes involved.

Work Related Non-advanced Further Education Planning

		Budget Process	
Date	*WRNAFE Planning with TC*	*Planning*	*Budget*
1987 September	Planning guidance issued by TC for 1988-89 plans. First formal meeting (TC/LEA Planning Team).	1988-89 Budget prepared on basis of historical cost plus adjustments for developments.	
October	Course starts determined. Programme revised/confirmed.		
December	Second formal meeting. Planning Team begins preparation of 88-89 Plan.		
1988 January	First draft of plan to TC. Third formal meeting.		
February	Planning Team. Amendments to draft.		
March	Submit plan to TC.		
April	Fourth formal meeting Planning Team. Planning agreed and approved. Second monitoring review of current programme (87-88).		
September		1988-89 academic year commences.	
October		FESR return. Numbers determined.	Planned budget determined for 1989-90 FTE numbers.

Nov. 88–March 89	Three year rolling total provision plan updated (89-90) (WRNAFE and other courses).	
April 1989	Projected FTE students agreed.	Colleges begin 1989-90 financial year.
September	1989-90 academic year commences.	Colleges advised of projected adjustments to 1990 financial year.
October	FESR returns actual FTE student numbers determined.	Colleges advised of planned budget for 1990-91.
November	WRNAFE plan revised in light of actual course starts/enrolments.	
Nov. 89–Mar. 90	Three year rolling total provision plan updated (1989-92).	
1990 April, November	Repeat above process.	Colleges begin 1990-91 financial year. Colleges advised of projected adjustments to 1991-92. Repeat proces above.

The Authority already had an extensive in-service programme before the onset of grant-related in-service training. Thus an INSET Advisory Committee constituted under the Teachers' Consultative Committee had been in place for several years.

In the summer of 1986, the Education Committee approved a paper from the Director of Èducation outlining the nature of the scheme and recommending that a proposal be prepared. They received a detailed 'policy for INSET' which had been drawn up by the Advisory Committee. A detailed plan was then produced by advisory staff based on advisory perceptions of need, a survey of schools and colleges, and the views of teachers' associations and regional INSET providers. These national aspects were managed by an Assistant Education Officer having responsibility for specific grant projects. The preparation of the LEAGTS proposal required a great deal of advisory time during the months of July and September 1986. The proposal was submitted at the beginning of October 1986 and notification of the outcome was received by Christmas 1986, just three months before the start of the 1987-88 financial year in which the scheme was to operate. The final scheme was approved by Education Committee in January 1987.

The secrets of successful planning demonstrated in this appendix are:

(*a*) to start early and build on existing curriculum policies;
(*b*) to build in the administrative and management costs;
(*c*) to meet the criteria in a way which anticipates local needs;
(*d*) to have effective mechanisms for consulting the clients;
(*e*) to be responsive to change with as much flexibility built in as possible;
(*f*) to ascribe sufficient staff time to the job;
(*g*) to have an effective senior management team to ensure that the advisory and administrative divisions work closely together;
(*h*) to be aware of the need for monitoring and evaluation of what is to be provided;
(*i*) to lay the ground work for a comprehensive INSET data processing system which can become part of the data base shared between the LEA and schools in local financial management.

7

Administration and School Management

INTRODUCTION

For many users the most important and useful function of a computer is its capacity to perform routine administrative tasks efficiently and quickly. The most obvious form of this capacity involves the paperflow of correspondence, internal memos, duty rotas, lists, statistical analyses and projections, stock management, and so on, that are characteristic of the modern office. Clearly, schools face tasks similar to these, but they are normally carried out by hand, usually by a senior teacher who spends all his or her time trying to keep on top of the paperwork.

The purpose of this chapter is to introduce and discuss the ways in which the computer might be used to assist in these time-consuming tasks of school administration. It is accepted, to begin with, that it will not be possible to become deeply involved in some of the associated technical issues, since they can be very complicated indeed. As well as this, only a reader who has experienced the difficulties—for example, of trying to produce a school timetable—can have a proper understanding of the problem. For the school principal or vice principal, who wishes to go further than is possible in one chapter of this sort, the book by Bird (1984) is strongly recommended.

There are a number of senses in which the computer can be used as an aid to administration in education, although not all of these receive equal attention in the literature devoted to the subject. The most obvious use, and the one that we shall be focusing upon in this chapter, is in regard to the administrative tasks normally carried out by the school office. However, we also wish, for a moment, to widen this notion of administration to include a consideration of two other aspects of its meaning. The first of these relates to curriculum planning, and in particular to its logistical and structural aspects. By this we refer to such things as the availability of subjects and corresponding specialist teachers, decisions about options, the organization of pupil-groups and bands, the allocation of laboratory space, resource analysis, and so on. It is not always realized that the transfer of a carefully thought out curriculum philosophy into a realized practical model requires a sophisticated and imaginative analysis of these infrastructural variables. The computer can be of enormous advantage in this highly technical and complicated work.

The third aspect of computer-based management which we wish to refer to briefly is the structuring and organization of resources, learning experiences, and time, within the classroom. Much modern analysis of education refers to the richness of the classroom environment as a miniature social world, a world which demands a wide range of judgemental and administrative skills, and suggests that the teacher must develop complex management systems to take account of this. The skills involved include such things as individualization of learning, keeping records of progress and of difficulties, ensuring that perceived particular social needs are provided, generating advice about future activity, and so on. To make it possible to begin to accomplish all this, the modern teacher is expected to add to his or her normal skills those of a manager, and those of an action researcher. The computer may help to make some aspects of this possible.

These three aspects of computer-based educational administration can be summarized as follows:

(*a*) The role of the computer in the running of the school office, or 'school administration';

(*b*) The use of statistical and logistical information as an aid to curriculum planning and analysis, or 'curriculum management';

(*c*) The management of the individual classroom, or 'classroom management'.

SCHOOL ADMINISTRATION

This is the most highly developed aspect of the three areas, with a fairly long history of progress, first with mainframe computers, and more recently with microcomputers. It is the one with which the rest of this section will be concerned. However, although useful procedures have been available on mainframes for some years to help with such tasks as timetabling, they have not been much taken up by schools, for the obvious reason that communication with mainframes requires circuitous and time-consuming procedures. For example, 'batch processing' was the normal communication method used until quite recently, and this involved preparing material on paper first, and then sending it to the computer centre where it was punched on cards which were then fed into the computer. Such a process compares badly in many respects with the modern on-line direct-interaction process.

Another difficulty in the way of general progress has been the conservative nature of schools and of school principals, who on the whole are not trained as administrators and who are therefore forced to learn their management techniques from experience. This means that each school is likely to have built up a set of techniques and procedures unique to itself, but often concerning the solution of the same set of basic administrative problems. This situation is further encouraged by the fact that, until recently, most schools were comparatively small and so could get by without very complex management techniques.

The software needed to begin to develop a school administration system on a microcomputer is only now becoming available, so those schools who wished to use a computer in the recent past were forced to begin to develop the software on their own. This led over time to the existence of a large number of individualized systems of varying scale and quality. Eventually some of these began to become available commercially, while at the same time other systems with their origins in mainframe computers also began to be available. The result is that there is now on the market a number of more-or-less comprehensive systems which will run on the machines most found in schools. The only problem facing the school is the evaluation and choice of one of these.

The distinction between, on the one hand, a large and increasing variety and number of home-made systems and, on the other, a professionally produced commercial system, has led to a debate about the relative merits of the two approaches. The supporters of local initiative argue that all schools are unique, with their own systems and their own history, and that even if a commercial system were bought, it would still have to be customized for the particular school. Others feel that schools should be encouraged to buy commercial systems arguing that the constant reproduction of a unique local system amounts to a waste of time and resources, and that the finished product is unlikely to work as well or as efficiently as the tried and tested commercial version. It is also argued that a local system may solve problems within a school in a piecemeal and incoherent way, and that good practice in the maintenance and testing of data may not be instituted.

Although there is no consensus about this problem, it is fairly well agreed that, whichever approach is chosen, a great deal of thought and planning and consultation is necessary before any decisions can be made. Consultation should be both internal and external. A staff team should be created and all colleagues should be kept in touch with developments. External advice should be sought from those schools with experience in the area. For example, visits can be made to schools which have purchased or constructed systems. These can be looked at in action and advice sought from those involved about pitfalls and difficulties. If all of this is done, it should then be possible to produce a careful and informed plan for the introduction and use of a computer system to meet the school's administrative needs. The final proposal should then be presented to colleagues for discussion.

It is also necessary to consider a variety of human issues which may be affected by the introduction of a computerized system. It is for this reason, among others, that a period of negotiation with staff about the consequences and effects of the system is suggested, so that they are reassured about the difficulties. This may involve arranging for teachers to visit schools where a system is already at work, so that they can talk to teachers who have grown used to a computerized system and hear their views about its use and its effects.

Teachers will worry about such things as the cost of the system, and the effect of this on the overall school budget, and about its effect on their own resource needs. They will also worry about the computer creating more work for them, about possible loss of status if the computer takes work away from them, and, perhaps more importantly, about being excluded from decision making. There is also some evidence to suggest that some teachers are afraid that computers will show them up as incompetent in that it will do some of their work more efficiently than they can. All of these fears and worries ought to be taken seriously and attempts made to understand and deal with them.

Finally, as a result of this preparation, a set of questions can be prepared and used to help in the evaluation of any proposed system. This might include asking such questions as:

Does the system meet the general needs of the school?
Is the system cost-effective with respect to time and human resources?
Is the system flexible enough to allow for the incorporation of new problems?
Is there a sensible and feasible system of data-capture and data input?
Is there a technical back-up service available to solve problems?
Is the system under continual development by its producers, and are revised versions received as a matter of course?

Answers to questions like these, and others, will help to ensure that the system chosen will be of some value to the school, and that it will make things better in the sense of more efficient, faster, more accurate, and so on.

If we now assume that a system has been bought and installed, there are then a number of aspects of its day-to-day operation that require consideration. To begin with, it is necessary to develop a routine for such things as: the creation of files; the updating of files; the security of files; the collection and input of data; the generation and distribution of output; and so on. This routine should be established and carried out by a group or team of staff, including one of the clerical staff. In particular it is unwise to leave to the staff enthusiast, mainly because if he or she leaves the school then no-one else will know the details of the operation, but also because one individual will not necessarily reflect the overall needs of the school.

The range of administrative tasks which the computer has been used for in schools is very large and includes such obvious things as timetabling, pupil records, word-processing, accounts, library, and examinations. It also includes such unexpected topics as transport, meals and parent interviews. We will now look at some of these in detail, drawing to some extent on the book by Bird (1984).

TIMETABLING

It is clearly not possible for a computer to produce a school timetable without a great deal of preliminary thought, preparation and data collection on the part of the people involved. But even when this is done the chances are that the data collected do not have a single first-time solution in the form of a timetable. This means that, as the work goes on, anomalies and impossibilities appear which involve judgement and compromise on how to alter the data. Even when this is done, the best that the computer can do is to produce a major draft, as a consequence of a series of interactions between the machine and the timetabler. Bird writes:

> Whether it will ultimately be possible to hand the whole process over to a microcomputer must remain a matter for debate.

The first decisions regarding the timetable are educational ones, and they result from negotiations and decisions made by the staff and the principal. These are based on the school 'philosophy of education', but they will also take account of previous experience and the detailed 'practitioner's knowledge' about the school held by the staff. Ideally decisions at this stage should also be informed by the logistical details related to the school's manpower resources, range of options, and so on. The generation of this data, if done by hand, can however be a complicated and time-consuming business, and they will not always be immediately available in an up-to-date and usable form. However, the use of this approach represents a second level of curriculum analysis, and this is what we have referred to earlier as 'curriculum management' and we will discuss later how the computer might be used in this curriculum-building stage.

Once the educational decisions about the structure of the school curriculum have been made, the next stage is the generation of a great deal of data about the proposed structure. When this is done there is then available software which can be used to assist and guide in various aspects of the preliminary work. Included in this is manpower and resource analysis, checking data for inconsistencies, and generating information about conflicts or clashes. The results of this kind of analysis are helpful although they do involve spending some time on data capture and input.

The next stage is the actual timetable construction and, depending on which package is used, this is done by the computer in a variety of different ways. Most modern packages, however, involve a series of revised versions or structured steps which allow the timetabler to feed in new or amended data, or to impose new constraints. As this process continues the drafts get closer and closer to an acceptable solution.

If this stage is successfully reached the advantages are then very great indeed. The computer will print out complete timetables, individualized staff and class timetables, day timetables, and any subsection of the overall timetable required. It will provide information about free periods, staff not on duty, and so on. Bird quotes from LAMSAC (1978) on the advantages as follows:

Better use of resources (teachers, specialist rooms, etc.) saving time for timetabling staff so that they may give more attention to other essential duties. A thoroughly checked timetable with full or part copies for all concerned.

Less stress on the timetabler.

An option structure better suited to demand.

A teaching staff more informed on general timetabling possibilities and difficulties and the need for planning.

PUPIL RECORDS

One of the unending tasks of school administration is the production of lists of pupils with such information as names, class marks, attendance records, and so on. This has to be done with reference to such things as, which class they belong to, or which set, or which year. Clearly a well-organized database of pupil records would make this task easier and less frustrating. It would also be likely to produce more accurate and up-to-date information. There are associated legal issues and the Data Protection Act, 1985 must also be taken into account.

There are a number of important decisions to be made before such a system is established. Perhaps the most important of these is the type of information to be recorded, i.e., exactly what data about each pupil are to be used. This decision must be informed by understanding and thought about a number of questions including the following:

What is the capacity of the machine being used?

Can the data be collected easily?

How often will the data need to be updated?

Are there social issues, such as confidentiality, involved in collecting and recording any of the data?

A typical list of entries to a pupil record file proposed by MUSE (see glossary) was as follows:

Field 1	Surname
Field 2	Forename or initials
Field 3	Tag to distinguish identical names

Field 4	Date of birth (YYMMDD)
Field 5	Sex
Field 6	Form/Tutor group
Field 7	House

This list could of course be made much longer by including additional information such as subjects being studied, date of entry, previous school, and so on. The home address is another possibility, but although it seems on first sight to be an important piece of information, Bird argues against its use on the grounds that it involves a lot of time to enter, takes up a lot of memory, and is actually used very little indeed. In general the amount of information to be stored on each pupil will depend crucially on the memory and storage restraints of the system being used.

So, before beginning, it is necessary to decide how many such records the school computer can handle in a sensible way. The next thing to look at is the set of tasks which such a database might be used to accomplish. Bird suggests, among others, the generation of an alphabetical school roll, a set of year rolls, house rolls, class lists, tutor-group lists, and so on; then the tedious task of generating school statistics for returns to Local Authority and to government departments; and, if the appropriate information has been stored, there is the analysis and listing of information about options. There is also the generation of reports on pupils based on subject choices, and the other tasks can be attempted if a carefully designed pupil database has been constructed.

It is also necessary to consider the problem of data capture. For example, if the system tries to deal with the daily roll-call, it is necessary to collect the information each morning in some systematic way so that it can be fed into the machine and processed. Or if the system is to be used to prepare information about examination entrances, then at some stage the information must be collected and input. Obviously some thought must be given to this issue of data capture so that the procedures are both comprehensive and simple. The two most usual approaches are, firstly, the use of a carefully designed form which is used for all data capture; and, secondly, the use of mark-card sense readers, which is fast but prone to error.

When the system is established it is also possible to use it to begin the generation of a careers file based on the collection and collation of the careers aspirations of pupils. When this is established, the data can be processed and used for such tasks as the facilitation of job placements.

WORD-PROCESSING

There is already a complete chapter on the use of word-processing in the classroom as a contribution to teaching and learning, but here we wish simply to refer to its usefulness in administration. To begin with there is the generation of form letters, that is letters which are used quite often in the course of a year. Normally these are produced by using stencils, making many copies, and then typing in the name of the recipient. With a word-processor such letters need to be typed once only and then stored on disk. They can then be recalled when needed, personalized with a name and a date, and used as often as is necessary. However, if a longer duplication run is involved then it is worth pointing out that using a word-processor can be a very inefficient method.

A similar process can be used for producing such documents as examination papers, booklists, class handouts, curriculum material, and so on. Once typed in and stored, they can be retained, updated when necessary and reproduced as required.

Most schools also produce yearly guides and booklets for parents, pupils and staff, and again these need to be typed once only and then stored on disk. Each year, or when needed, a (revised) master copy can be produced for printing, or a stencil for duplication. In this way the seemingly endless production and reproduction of school documents can be made faster, more up-to-date and more accurate.

LIBRARY

Although we are here concerned mainly with discussing how the computer can help with the administration of a school library, it is important to remember that the arrival of computers, and information technology generally, has made possible a revision and rethinking of the range and variety of tasks which the library can be used to accomplish. This much more complicated general topic is not our concern here.

From the single vantage of library administration it is immediately clear that the generation of computer-based library datafiles has the potential to become a very wide-ranging curriculum aid. For this to be so the computer record has to be very carefully designed in the first place so that educationally useful data can be extracted. At the same time the memory and processing limitations of the computer system being used must be borne in mind.

One way to approach this is to consider what sort of output staff and pupils might find useful. For example a group of pupils may be doing a project on butterflies. Ideally the system ought to make it possible to generate a list of books, magazines, and other library resources which contain information about butterflies. Similarly a teacher may wish to design a set of lessons on architecture and again the computer ought to able to search its records with respect to this keyword. This means that the design of the record for each entry must contain some information in a form that allows for this.

The development of a system to perform a task as complicated and wide-ranging as these examples may be beyond the resources of all school libraries as it involves both the initial task of creating the datafile, and the ongoing task of updating it. However, it may be possible to cooperate with another school or set of schools in some of this work, and in particular in the cataloguing process. In the end, if a system is carefully designed and organized then its usefulness is hard to exaggerate. Not only can it be used as a teaching and learning resource, but it can also be used to help pupils to develop information and study skills.

8

The Management of Educational Plant and Resources

Section 8 of the Education Act, 1944 lays upon the Local Education Authority the duty to secure provision of primary and secondary schools:

> It shall be the duty of every local education authority to secure that there shall be available for their area sufficient schools (*a*) for providing primary education . . ., (*b*) for providing secondary education . . ., and the schools available for an area shall not be deemed to be sufficient unless they are sufficient in number, character and equipment to afford for all pupils opportunities for education offering such variety of instruction and training as may be desirable in view of their different ages, abilities and aptitudes . . . .

Section 41 of the Act lays on LEAs the duty to provide adequate facilities for Further Education, that is to say:

(*a*) full-time and part-time education for persons over compulsory school age, and
(*b*) leisure time occupation in such organized cultural training and recreative activities as are suited to their requirements, for any persons over compulsory school

age who are able and willing to profit by the facilities provided for that purpose.

It is to be noted that the Act does not impose on LEAs the duty of providing all the schools necessary to enable them to discharge the duty imposed by Section 8. Indeed, most careful and detailed consideration is given in the Act to the provision of voluntary schools (mainly by the churches) and to the use which may be made by an authority of independent (or private) schools. The fact remains that by far the greater number of schools are provided by the LEA; and it is of interest to speculate whether anyone involved in drafting the Bill which became the great Act of 1944, or involved in its passage through the House of Commons, had any idea of the scale of school building which would be required to carry out the duty imposed by Section 8.

In fact, it launched the education service on an operation bigger than any seen in any other part of the public sector; an operation which far outstripped the great wave of educational building which followed the Education Act of 1870. The growth in the number of children born in the post-war years, reinforced, in some parts of the country, by numbers of immigrant children and everywhere by the raising of the school leaving age to 15 and then in 1973 to 16, established school and college building as a major part of the work of all education offices. For nearly 40 years it has been one of the pressure points in educational administration as authorities have struggled against the calendar, and sometimes even against the clock, to keep up with rising school and college rolls.

It has to be remembered that education is the only one of the public services where the law requires a place to be provided for every member of its client group so far, at least, as the provision of schools is concerned. We may have as many prisons, as many hospitals, as many old people's homes, and as many houses as at any moment society believes it can afford and, if the supply falls short of meeting the demand, so be it. We shall do better gradually over the years. But where schools are concerned every child presented by his parents must be accommodated at least until he has reached the leaving age of

16. The effort needed to achieve this has been immense; the accumulated expertise, educational, financial and architectural, which is now a common feature of all education authorities, is unique in the public service. The country can justly be proud of what has been achieved and the great number of teachers, administrators and politicians who from all parts of the world, come to visit our schools are an indication of the international recognition of those achievements.

But now things have changed, not least as a result of the demographic trends which produced an initial dramatic fall in primary school numbers. While they are recovering (but not to their previous levels) the numbers in secondary schools continue to decline. In the post-16 sector, Government initiatives to control the number of students have affected establishments in the public and private sectors. Furthermore, contraction is in part, at least, responsible for a number of other developments which are affecting and will affect the design and equipping of educational buildings. These include for example, the wider development of nursery education, the most effective ways of developing/remodelling secondary schools to serve merged schools and the needs of the modern curriculum, the development of comprehensive education, wider community use of schools, the need to cope with areas of educational and social disadvantage, the requirements of the 1981 Education Act concerning special educational need and, of course, the intervention of the MSC via the TVEI pilot schemes and the YTS for 16+ young people. It is obvious that all these new factors, together with the strains imposed on the system by the 'opting out' clauses of the 1988 Act make the management of educational plant and resources a very different matter from the expansionary requirements of a rapidly growing school population between 1945-71, when the pre-eminence of what is termed 'basic need' i.e., the provision of 'roofs over heads was virtually the sole gauge of capital investment in educational buildings and resources.

To set the scenario for this chapter, it is important to devote some time to a more detailed consideration of falling rolls, and the surplus places which this phenomenon produces. 'Contraction' may seem negative and pessimistic in terms of educational development, but it offers opportunities for education reform and development at least as great if not greater than the rapid 'expansion' of educational institutions and resources managed so wonderfully well between 1945 and 1971. In the second half of that 'expansion' period, significant advances were made in the design of new secondary schools to meet the needs of comprehensive secondary education as an alternative to compressing children of all abilities into the existing and often inadequate grammar and secondary modern school buildings designed for a bi-partite, selective system of secondary education. Equally, great strides were made between 1961 and 1971 in the design of more versatile new primary school buildings, eliminating unecessarily lengthy corridors, assisting teachers and children to work together in more flexible, open groupings than was really possible in the single teacher, single class group, cellular classrooms designed with the objectives of the 1870 Education Act in mind rather than present day objectives. Even though the task of making the nation literate and numerate was thought to have been substantially completed before the Second World War, the method of training teachers allied to public and parental expectations based on the education they had experienced, ensured that generally new educational plant was reproduced up to 1945 with little design alteration. Much progress has been made throughout the country in redesigning new educational plant since 1945, due in no small measure to the work of the Architects and Buildings Branch of the then Ministry of Education. Nevertheless, much remains to be done in remodelling existing schools and in designing new schools to take account of all the new factors mentioned earlier in this chapter. With far more limited capital resources available we need to ensure the most versatile and efficient use of materials, furniture and equipment to enable new curriculum development to take place.

Falling rolls and surplus places call for careful management of educational plant and resources which could bring about improvements in the way in which the LEA fulfils its legal obligation to meet the needs of the population of its area. It has been estimated that nationally the total school population of England and Wales may fall from approximately 9 million in 1979 to about 7.5 million by 1990. Within this national picture there will be much local variation. In some cases there will be a permanent fall as people migrate from the area; in others the fall will be followed by a rise in due course as a consequence of the birth-rate; in some areas there may, by a combination of factors, be a net gain in population. The effects of new housing developments have to be gauged carefully to try to judge whether the number and type of houses will result in overall increases in the school population or to internal migration, both within and between individual school populations. Each LEA must therefore carefully plan and forecast the needs not only of the total area, but also of individual localities within its area.

The effect of recent government legislation, which increased parental choice and limited the control over annual admission limits that the 1980 Education Act had allowed local authorities to exercise, is likely to make such forward planning far more difficult.

In planning, the administrator must have regard primarily to demographic factors, but these will be very radically influenced by social, educational and financial considerations. Financially, the case for closing schools or taking surplus places out of use is compelling. The Department of Education and Science estimated that for every 100,000 places taken out of use savings of approximately £10 million could be made—excluding savings on teacher salaries. If savings made on the heating, lighting and other maintenance costs of buildings could be applied to other elements of the service improvements in the provision of resources such as books and equipment could be looked for. While the full extent of such benefits does not always accrue to the LEA, it is nonetheless detrimental to crucial educational provision if money is unnecessarily expended on maintaining surplus places.

Increased resources are not the only educational benefits which might be looked for. Closure of small schools could lead to the transfer of children to larger schools where, for example, multi-age groups could be eliminated, a larger range of curriculum options could be offered, better technical and craft amenities could be enjoyed and obsolete buildings not well suited to modern needs could be dispensed with. At the sixth form level concentration of pupils into fewer, larger units has obvious advantages. These are some of the factors which the administrator will bear in mind when reviewing the provision of buildings and resources.

Social factors also are important. Accessibility of schools must, as always, require careful consideration. Long fatiguing journeys will not be good for children or acceptable to parents. Crossing of busy roads—particularly by young children—is dangerous and undesirable. It may therefore not be feasible for the LEA to close some small schools and, indeed, the Government has begun to recognize this fact. Schools are more than the sum of places that they provide. Parents hold schools in esteem and reinforce their views by seeking to secure the admission of their children to those schools. Reasons for parental preferences are diverse—not solely related to examination success. Some schools are by design community schools catering for the interests and involvement of the community they serve. Others are community schools by tradition and local acceptance. Some indeed are the focal point of the social and cultural life of the area. All these factors must be in the mind of those managing buildings and resources when they contemplate taking them out of use. This will frequently involve a nice balance of judgment before reaching a decision, particularly in view of the provision of the 1988 Act which strengthens the ability of the community to make choices.

The Act requires the admission limits of schools to be set at a level not lower than they are physically capable of accommodating using an admission level not lower than their standard number, as defined by the admissions to the school in 1979 or for schools established since 1979 (i.e. subject to the publication of Notices under Section 12 or 13 of the 1980 Act) the number fixed when they came into being. The Act also gives governors increased powers, including the right to appeal to the Secretary of State to be allowed to change the standard number. The consequences of this legislation for less popular schools and the communities they serve will pose new problems for the administrator and further inhibit the application of any form of planning which attempts to make the best use of resources for the overall benefit of an Authority's clients.

To close a school or to reduce the number of places in a school, the LEA must publish its proposals in accordance with Section 12 or Section 15 of the 1980 Act. Objections to those proposals may be submitted to the LEA by ten or more local government electors for the area within two months of their publication. These must be transmitted to the Secretary of State who must take them into account in deciding whether to approve the authority's proposals. Despite indications from the DES that the Secretary of State would do his best to expedite the formal procedures, there is often a considerable lapse of time between the expression of the need for action because of falling rolls and the carrying out of necessary action.

The DES requires that consultations should take place before any notices are published. Good public relations are essential at every stage: all concerned, governors, staff of the affected schools, parents and the general public of the area should be given the opportunity of being acquainted with the facts and the bases of decisions. Objections to proposals to close schools have generated a substantial volume of case law, particularly with respect to the amount of detail that has to be given to interested parties in the consultation process. It is now accepted that consultations based on a number of options are not sufficient; detailed proposals of the exact intentions must be made clear. This inevitably leads to the need for a number of rounds of consultations before the actual proposals are published in the form of public notices.

Falling rolls and the consequent management of plant require the concentrated exercise of many skills which are referred to more extensively in another chapter—sound statistical information, thorough understanding of the geographical area and of educational issues, political and social awareness, ability to balance delicate matters and to formulate reasoned conclusions, power to communicate and the power of setting out salient facts clearly and concisely. The extent of the consultative processes and the timescale required for the publication and implementation of notices can be a cause of great strain and uncertainty for teachers and parents, so above all the administrator must have a patient and sympathetic understanding of the many personal problems that will inevitably arise from any school closure or reduction of school places and which may well come directly to him for resolution.

At this point, it is important to glance back in time at what is still the legislative cornerstone of our educational system, the 1944 Education Act. Section 11 of that Act required each LEA to prepare and submit to the Secretary of State a Development Plan for Primary and Secondary Schools showing the action which the authority proposed to take to see that there should be sufficient primary and secondary schools available for its area and the successive measures by which it proposed to accomplish that purpose. The section also prescribed very carefully the nature of what was clearly intended to be a most detailed and thorough examination of the educational needs of the nation. Each LEA's Development Plan (and there was one also required for Further Education entitled 'A Scheme for Further Education and Plan for County Colleges') was of inestimable value and the major guideline for the development of educational institutions during the expansionary period up till the early 1960s. It has perhaps slipped into desuetude since that date, but nonetheless it is clear that every LEA must continually review the provision of buildings and other resources to meet the constantly changing needs of the population of its area.

Fundamentally it matters not whether the thoughts of 1947 are the same as those of today. What matters is that education authorities came to recognize the value of a Development Plan in one form or another. Such a plan needs constant up-dating and revision but it should exist to provide the essential framework within which the planning of individual schools can be undertaken.

In creating that framework, the authority must necessarily identify its needs in some detail—its need to build to meet basic need (i.e., the need to put roofs over the heads of children who would otherwise be without a school place); its need to build for the reorganization of secondary education; its need to replace the worst of the worn-out primary schools, many of them more than 100 years old! Basic need has always been with us and continues to be so in some areas of new housing. After a decade of falling birthgroups, the recent upturn in some areas, though not to previous high levels, will mean that inevitably the meeting of basic need must remain the permanent first priority. The importance of other types of need has varied over the last 40 years, and has reflected the changing emphasis which successive governments have attached to the different aspects of education development. For, given the constraints upon the national purse, priorities there must always be, and, in broad outline at any rate, they must be determined nationally.

The chosen mechanism of central government control has been the approved building programme, generally an affair of annual allocation but occasionally an attempted three-year rolling programme designed to help authorities to plan ahead with a greater measure of certainty. Unfortunately, this has almost invariably had to be withdrawn during the three-year cycle as a result of financial crisis.

In inviting submissions by authorities (whether of single or three-year programmes) central government has indicated the types of project acceptable at that particular moment. At the end of the Second World War, priority went to projects for repair and re-building of bomb-damaged schools; in 1947 raising of the school leaving age was a major preoccupation. In 1960-65 the emphasis switched to the elimination of all-age schools and the provision of accommodation in secondary schools for science and technical studies. From 1968 onwards programmes were devoted to the improvement of conditions in inner city schools. For three years from 1971, there was a modest attempt to replace worn-out primary schools, and the raising of the school leaving age to 16 took place in 1972. From 1974 onwards nursery programmes were established following the White Paper 'A Framework for Expansion'; in 1977-79 there were programmes of special projects to aid the reorganization of secondary education and, since 1979, there has been emphasis laid on the development of facilities in schools in areas of special educational and social need and, more recently, projects that will enable surplus places to be taken out of use or to replace buildings which, after a long period of poor levels of maintenance, are rapidly becoming dangerous.

In this way, the major building programme has acted not only as a financial regulator but as a steering mechanism ensuring, as governments have come and gone, that the truly massive resources ploughed into school building have promoted their policies—political as well as educational.

It is a common misconception that, in allocating to an authority a building programme of a certain value, central government is 'granting' the authority that amount of money. In fact, an allocation by way of a building programme is nothing more than a permission to spend that sum of money. It guarantees that approval to borrow money (in layman's terms to take out a mortgage) will be forthcoming.

The basis on which bids and resulting allocations are made was fundamentally altered in the light of the new capital expenditure control arrangements introduced by the Local Government Planning and Land Act, 1980. Previously, each government department was responsible for making a separate and self-contained allocation to each local government service and so far as the education service was concerned, this was based on very detailed bids for individual projects. The 1980 Act changed the whole concept of control of capital expenditure and, while involving new and more complex procedures, did in fact give a greater degree of freedom to local authorities to plan their overall capital programmes. It is important to understand the principal innovations introduced by this Act.

First and foremost, allocations of what is known as 'prescribed' expenditure—broadly speaking expenditure on the acquisition, construction and improvement of land, buildings and plant—are made in five main blocks to local authorities. These comprise education, housing, transport, personal social services and other services. Though these block allocations are still announced separately, once they have been made local authorities are free to spend them as they choose and to vire them between services. They are also free to augment them in two ways. They may overspend an allocation by 10 per cent in one year and this may then be carried forward to the following year provided it does not exceed 10 per cent of that year's allocation. Conversely, they may underspend the year's allocation by 10 per cent and carry forward the underspend on the same understanding that the sum carried forward is not more than 10 per cent of the following year's allocation. More importantly, however, and this is a very significant element in an authority's freedom to plan its capital programmes, it may enhance its government allocation by the use of a prescribed proportion (as low as 30 per cent in some years) of capital receipts that it has accrued by sale of existing building stock or land.

The method of controlling capital expenditure was also fundamentally altered by the Act and it is now based on the total of capital payments that may be made within each financial year rather than on the value of work started within that year. Traditionally, under the old system, provided a project had actually started, or the contract had been signed before the 1 April of the starts year, it did not matter how much or how little of the total cost was incurred within that year. Under the new system of control payments rather than starts are critical.

To try to increase the amount of capital that they are permitted to spend, authorities have made various attempts over the years to use creative accounting, particularly in respect of arrangements for leasing and deferred purchase. Not surprisingly successive items of legislation have been introduced to limit such opportunities. In addition, there has been an increase in the amount of central control of some educational expenditure, through Educational Support Grants. The capital consequences of these, whether in respect of the LEA's contribution or that funded by Central Government, have all to be set against the Authority's capital allocation, thus limiting the amount remaining for other purposes.

The annual allocations show approved spending limits for three years: the first year consists of a figure that includes within it the aggregate of all expenditure committed from projects started in earlier years as well as an allocation designed to enable new projects to start; the following two years give an indication of expenditure that will be committed as a result of projects that will not have been completed in the first year but they do not represent a guarantee of future years' allocations. In other words, if an authority wishes to start a £1 million project in Year 1 without a guarantee that its allocation for Years 2 and 3 will be adequate for the project to be completed, it can only do so if it is confident that funds from capital receipts or virement will enable the completion of the project should the government allocation be inadequate.

The new system requires the local education authority to show in its annual submission to the Department of Education and Science both its spending plans and its outstanding committed expenditure from previous years. Similarly the local authority as a whole must make overall calculations for the whole range of its services, unless it has continued to regard government allocations as self-contained for each separate service. If it has exercised any degree of virement between service or has used any of its own capital receipts to enhance its spending limits then it clearly must keep a careful account of its total spending patterns.

The new arrangements are considerably more complex than those they superseded, insofar as they require close and regular monitoring not only of the progress of individual projects but of the actual payment of accounts, since—and this has to be emphasized—payments rather than work completed are the critical factor in the new procedures. Delays and slippage of projects for whatever reason—be it difficulties in acquiring land, changes in political decisions, delay in approvals by the Secretary of State, staff illness, etc.—can seriously affect spending patterns, and if projects are not quickly substituted as the need arises and payments for completed work are not expedited, then capital allocations may be underspent by more than the 10 per cent tolerance referred to earlier. This could have the consequent effect of requiring greater use to be made of, say, capital receipts in the following years.

Conversely, however, the advantages of the new system are that it enables the individual authority to plan its capital spending as a whole; to decide its overall priorities within the totality of funds available from the two sources, i.e., government allocation and capital receipts; and to avoid the traditional scramble to get work started by the 1 April each year. It may well seem to those operating the system on a day-to-day basis that similar freedom could have been achieved with less complex procedures to be observed but nevertheless the overall flexibility the individual authority now has to plan its capital programmes is to be welcomed.

Unfortunately, so far as the education service is concerned, there is a further complexity that does not apply to other services and that lies in the procedures relating to capital expenditure at voluntary aided and special agreement schools. These are separate from those relating to all other educational expenditure but are nevertheless under the aegis of the education authority.

In brief, the governors of aided and special agreement schools must submit their requests for all improvement projects costing less than £2,500 directly to the DES for an allocation under its rationing scheme. All their requests for improvement projects costing more than £2,500 must be submitted to the local education authority for it to forward to the DES. The authority must indicate the extent of its support for such projects and make provision within its own capital allocation for those projects it is prepared to support and for such LEA contributions as are required. The allocation made by the DES for the voluntary schools is quite separate from that made to the authority for other educational capital work, but is announced on the same three-year basis described earlier, i.e., Year 1 comprising previously committed as well as new expenditure and Years 2 and 3 committed expenditure outstanding from Year 1. The allocation for the voluntary schools does not, however, include any expenditure on these schools for which the LEA is responsible and this must be met from within the authority's total 'prescribed' capital expenditure allocation.

The LEA is required to submit similar details about committed and planned new expenditure in respect of aided and special agreement schools as for its other educational projects but an added difficulty arises, insofar as the authority itself has little or no control over the progress of work at voluntary schools. In order to compile its submissions to the DES it has to obtain information from diocesan authorities and it must not overlook the existence of aided schools that are totally separate from any diocesan arrangements. (These are usually old-established grammar school foundations.)

So far as submission to the DES are concerned, these too have been fundamentally revised to take account of the greater freedom now vested in the local authority. Formerly, the Department called for very detailed annual returns of information in order to calculate the precise deficit of school places in growth areas, according to very specific criteria.

Information about basic need is still requested but in a less detailed form and confined to a brief statement of the total number of new places required over a planned three-year period, related to three age groups, 4-11, 11-16 and 16+. Authorities are asked to provide supporting information to help in the Department's analysis of the figures. So far as improvement projects are concerned, the Department takes account of the information it asks authorities to supply from time to time about the number of pupils accommodated in very old or unsatisfactory buildings—broadly pre-1903 primary and pre-1919 or substantially pre-1945 secondary building—and the number of pupils in areas of educational and social disadvantage. It also seeks information on the extent to which surplus places have been taken out of use and particular projects which will enable further places to be removed.

The forms on which this simplified information is requested would in themselves provide a very inadequate basis on which the Department could form a judgement about an individual authority's needs and it recognises this by suggesting that authorities may submit supporting information which they consider may be of assistance of the Department. It is clearly in the interests of individual authorities to do this, particularly if the DES allocation continues to play a significant part in the amount of capital building the authority is able to undertake.

In addition to its bids for primary and secondary schools, the LEA is asked to submit bids for other areas of the education service—nursery, special, further and higher education—though these are judged not on a formula basis but on their individual merits and needs.

When the DES announces the authority's allocation for the following year, on the three-year spending basis, it indicates how it has been built up by reference to the separate sectors of the service, namely schools, further and higher education. It makes it clear, however, that this is no more than a guide to the education authority: the disposition of the allocation is entirely a matter for the authority itself, which is also free to vire between the education block and any of the other capital expenditure blocks announced by the other government departments. It may in a sense seem anomalous that the DES should still be showing the separate elements of the education authority's allocation when the system has changed so fundamentally and it may well be that this procedure will itself be varied as the procedures take firmer root. For the time being, the separate break-down serves as an indication of the way in which the Department has judged the education authority's needs in the light of national policies.

As far as the capital programme is concerned there are two factors which impose constraints on the time-tabling of the building process. The first relates to the statutory approvals which are required whenever a local authority intends to establish a new school, ceases to maintain a school, or make a significant change in the character and size of a school. These regulations (Sections 12 and 13 of the 1980 Act) involve the local authority in the publication of Notices so that the Secretary of State may receive comments and objections upon proposals: the resultant timescale will vary significantly according to the nature of each proposal.

The second major influence on the timescale lies in the timing of capital allocations. The Notices require implementation dates to be stated but, as these may prove to be incompatible with the extent of the capital allocation in any one year, the planning process can be further complicated and preliminary design work may have to be done in the knowledge that it may eventually prove to be abortive.

In 1985, a report of the Efficiency Scrutiny of the DES's Architects and Buildings Group recommended that most LEA building projects should no longer be subject, as a matter of course, to professional examination and assessment by the staff of the A & B group. As a result, the limit for minor works was increased to £ 200,000 and simpler procedures now apply for major works costing less than £2 million.

For these, if not the subject of Section 12 or 13 notices, no submission is required. For those subject to Section 12 or 13 notices, Form ABBX has to be submitted at tender stage. This requires a short description of the project, details of the relevant Section 12 or 13 notices and an undertaking that the works will conform to the requirements of the Education (School Premises) Regulations, 1981 and to the Department's constructional standards as specified in AM2/85. It is intended that these projects will be approved after the receipt of the specified particulars, provided these are in order, without examination or assessment by the department's professional staff.

Where, for some reason, the Authority foresees difficulty in being able to meet the regulations and constructional standards on any major works the Department needs to be informed of the particular circumstances at the earliest possible stage. This requirement also applies to minor works projects, which otherwise require no formal approval. Where, however, a series of minor works is to be carried out at an establishment, and the sum of those works exceeds £200,000, then the submission requirements relating to major works must be met.

For projects costing in excess of £2 million, the accelerated approval procedure applies. This relates to cases where the Authority anticipates that the cost will fall within plus or minus 10 per cent of the appropriate net cost, calculated by reference to the guidelines. The appropriate forms, together with sketch plans have to be submitted and a gross cost agreed as a result of submission of tender details. At tender stage it is necessary to submit further information. If at that stage the gross cost is met and a certificate of undertaking can be provided, formal approval will be given without further discussion. If not, the gross tender cost will need to be specifically agreed with the Department.

The relaxation of the approval procedures does not, however, mean that an LEA has a totally free hand. Annex A to Circular 1/86 makes it clear that the Secretary of State attaches importance to the need for continuing dialogue between DES building professionals and officers of the LEAs in support of the achievement of value for money. For example, authorities are asked to look at alternative solutions to such problems as school closures to remove surplus places, including the cost of keeping schools open. In such instances it is likely that building work would still be required to bring existing buildings up to modern day standards, resulting in the need for additional architectural services and associated fees.

The Secretary of State also reserves the right to require the submission of additional information and to introduce professional appraisal of projects from an authority whose performance appears to him to fall consistently far below a reasonable standard of value for money. Accordingly, therefore, LEAs are asked to submit details on the appropriate ABB forms of all major projects for which formal approval procedures do not apply.

Automatic approval is not given to projects at voluntary aided schools, but voluntary bodies and/or governors of voluntary aided schools can seek 'accelerated approval' by agreeing a gross target cost with the Department prior to the submission of tender details. Formal approval would then be given without further discussion if the gross target cost were met on tender and the local education authority confirmed that the project complied with the Standards for School Premises Regulations and the Department's current recommended constructional standards.

The Education (School Premises) Regulations, 1981 represent the most recent version of regulations which first appeared in 1945. Minimum recreational areas, areas of playing fields, minimum interior areas of teaching accommodation, minimum numbers of sanitary fittings and washbasins, and more general regulations on the required provision for staff rooms, ancillary accommodation for staff and accommodation for meals are all laid down. Many of the requirements are expressed in terms of minima, but in a period of constantly escalating building costs minima more and more tend to be regarded as the most that can possibly be achieved. Thus it is that since the middle 1950s the architect has been more and more relentlessly ground down between the upper millstone of financial limitations and the nether millstone of minimum regulation requirements.

From what has gone before the reader might well have gained the impression that the Department of Education and Science is a restrictive, constraining body. This would be a travesty of the true position. As the agent of central government the department has a duty to monitor closely (which often means to limit) the cost of school building, always an unenviable job. It must ensure that minimum standards are achieved: a task which must be rigorously undertaken in the interests of educational, technical and hygiene standards. But these monitoring roles are but a part of its involvement in school building. Its more constructive functions should be recognized.

The Architects and Buildings Branch of the Department of Education and Science was first set up in 1949. Since then it has played a major development role in school building. Not only has it, over the years, scrutinized the plans of all authorities; but through development projects its own architects have cooperated with the architects of local authorities in planning and building schools and other education institutions to meet what have been seen as the needs of any particular moment. A secondary modern school, a grammar school, a rural 'open plan' school, nursery accommodation through adaptations of spare primary accommodation; these are but a few of the long list of projects, each of which has tried to find an answer to a widely felt need. And it should be stressed that what has been produced eventually has been offered only as one answer, not as the answer. The building bulletin which has followed each such project has described in both educational and technical terms the difficulties encountered as well as solutions proposed. The building bulletin on fire prevention in schools represents another type of publication from A and B Branch (as it is commonly known) which has been of immense importance to education authority architects. In the case of this bulletin it can fairly be said that to it must go much of the credit for the generally high safety standards of schools in this country.

Let us now return to the local authority facing up to its building project. In many authorities advanced planning may already have begun ahead of administrative approval. The vital process of briefing the architect, making clear to him the educational needs of the eventual user, may well have had to start much earlier if the separate and critical programmes of the architect and the treasurer are to be met.

Of all the many stages in the process of building a new school (or extending or rehabilitating an existing one) this is the most crucial. A vague or inadequate briefing is usually the sign of inadequate educational thinking. It is the surest recipe for an inadequate school. The educational administrator and the architect should each make his own contribution based on a clear and detailed understanding of the kind of school required. On the part of the architect this understanding goes far beyond the number of spaces to be provided. It calls for an understanding of the use to be made of each space and its relationships with other spaces, and of the nature of the educational experience which is to be offered to the pupil. It calls not only for the understanding of the technical but also the aesthetic ambience which is required. It calls for a knowledge of child development. In some authorities, standard briefs exist which should help the architect to develop an appreciation of the educationist's requirements. Initial briefs should reflect a philosophy of education, a commitment by the professional educator to a concept of the curriculum and the teaching and learning methods by which the aims of the curriculum are to be achieved. Both educationist and architect should be fully conscious of the importance of what they are doing. They are creating an environment which will have a major impact on the educational experiences of generations of children. Time spent on developing these briefs is crucial to the success of any operation. In meeting a planning programme or an occupation date 'corners' may be cut at a number of points; they should never be cut during the initial preparation and further development of any initial brief.

To this point, there has been little visible sign of anything that the layman would recognize as part of building a school. Now surely at last what he might well recognise as 'the real business' of school building—the drawing of plans—can begin. But is the site known and available? In terms of meeting programme dates, and the planned phasing of expenditure that is now critical, the availability of the site is of the utmost importance. The process of acquisition, the transfer of ownership and arrangements for purchase in themselves will take time. But where a site to be identified, where planning permissions have still to be obtained, and negotiations have to be begun perhaps with an unwilling vendor, then the eighteen months which normally elapse between the announcement of an allocation and a start on site may well prove to be inadequate.

The importance of forward planning and forward purchasing of sites is likely to be particularly great in the case of schools to be built in or near the centre of major urban areas. There the availability of land will be limited, competition from industry, housing and other public services for what is available will be fierce, and the education building programme may well be held up by the complications of other public programmes may well be held up by the complications of other public programmes such as clearance and redevelopment or major housing improvement schemes. In the extent of their forward planning, authorities have quite clearly varied enormously and it must be recognized that the problem of earmarking and acquiring sites has been easier where what has been involved has been a 'green field site'. In such cases to buy and hold a site for twenty or even thirty years has not been too difficult. To do the same thing in the middle of urban areas has been an entirely different kettle of fish.

When, despite the complications involved, the site has been identified and is in the authority's possession, then the time to elaborate on the initial brief and begin to produce sketch plans has at last arrived. Here again emphasis must be laid upon the value of architect and educationist working together as the first thinking begins to take shape on the drawing board. This is a stage when the advice and ideas of the local authority inspectorate or advisory service will be refined and when the views and experiences of practising teachers should be brought into consideration. The most successful planning is not likely to take place in a situation where, having handed over the brief, the educationist sees no more of the project until a finished sketch plan with an ABB2 plan analysis and outline specification appears on his desk. Exchange of ideas, a joint approach by educationist and architect, may lead not only to the most helpful solution to a problem; they may lead to the recognition of an unforeseen opportunity, a good idea which, working separately, neither educationist nor architect might have spotted. The path which leads between the architect's office and the Education Department should be one of the best trodden paths in country or city hall.

It is at sketch plan stage that many of the basic design decisions are made. Those which relate to the exterior include the location of the building on site, points and means of access to it for pedestrians and vehicles, means of connection from the proposed building to the services of the public utilities and the orientation of the building. Internally basic decisions have now to be made about the shape of various spaces, their relationships one to another, the circulation flows of children. These are but a few of the many questions which call for consideration at this early stage of design. What seems like the obvious solution to one problem may rule out the obvious solution to another; compromises will be inevitable at many points. Furthermore, compromises which overcome technical problems may well have a 'knock on' effect on the educational acceptability of the plan. This underlines the need for the involvement at this stage of the educationist.

Recent legislation has increased the governors' responsibilities. Where, therefore, work involves the extension, rehabilitation or straight replacement of an existing school, the governors and staff will rightly expect to be consulted when initial sketch plans have been prepared and at all subsequent stages of the design for a building that is likely to affect the curriculum and running costs of the school. The process is unlikely to be well carried out in haste.

Another path which should be equally well worn is that between architect's office and that of the quantity surveyor—a key person in the whole business of school building.

In terms of realistic, as distinct from inflated, expectations from the client (and even from the job architect) the quantity surveyor's close participation is invaluable. He must prepare a reliable budget figure with cash flow predictions which is sufficient to satisfy the brief and meet the programme. Costs may be established using data based on past experience or cost models previously agreed between the Education and Architect's Departments. Such costs need to be compatible with the value guidelines issued by the DES. The quantity surveyor's contribution must ensure that the scheme provides value for money, balancing initial costs with subsequent on-going costs and achieving a balance of expenditure throughout all elements of the project so that the distribution of resources reflects the needs of the brief (e.g., should more or less be spent on external works to the detriment or benefit of the building?). At least it should hold out the hope that the tenders, when received, will be reasonably close to the cost target which in turn prevents the hasty and often under-considered process of pruning plans at tender stage.

The temptation always exists to overcome technical or educational design difficulties by additional expenditure, so there is much to be said for the regular involvement of the quantity surveyor. What is reinforced at this stage of the design process is the extent to which educational, technical and financial considerations are interlocked, that a plan is an organic whole, rather than a series of loosely articulated parts, so that technical problems may well be financial and educational problems as well and that in many cases they will call for an inter-disciplinary solution. It is the complexity of the decision-making process that makes it imperative that the consequences of any changes suggested at the last minute, no matter how obviously good they appear to be, are very carefully thought through. Without such care, the very reason why a different decision was originally made, with its associated knock on effects, may be overlooked.

When sketch plans are available and initial costings determined, the procedures to be followed are as detailed earlier in this chapter.

Detailed layouts, showing the proposed position of fixed furniture, service points are then prepared. It is important, too, that layouts for the loose furniture are introduced at this stage, to ensure all the necessary furniture and equipment can, in fact, be accommodated. Working drawing can then commence. It is now vital that no further amendments are introduced, since they can prove very expensive in terms of time, fees and goodwill of the contract. Extensions and alterations affect the operation of an existing occupied building and need discussion between heads of establishments and the professional staff engaged on the development of the project. It is essential that the occupants know of the conditions that will prevail during construction and have accepted a method of operation which will be clearly described in the contract documents and allowed for by the contractor when preparing his tender. Stopping the progress of a contract for school examinations, for example, will be expensive if requested after the contract has been placed. Likewise, temporary boiler shutdown, alterations to kitchens and similar work should be arranged at periods to cause the minimum of inconvenience to the occupants. From here on, unless significant changes in the plans are proposed, the educationist retreats into the background, leaving progress to architect and quantity surveyor, since this stage of the operation is mainly a technical one. As working drawings develop, quantities are 'taken off' and a bill of quantities takes shape. The job is now moving towards tender stage.

Obviously the aim is to obtain the lowest possible satisfactory tender and to this end there are a number of different tendering procedures. Least sophisticated of all is the invitation of tenders from any contractor prepared to submit one. This leaves the authority open to the situation where a very low tender may be received from a contractor who has not the capacity, either financial or organizational, to carry out the work. It can also lead to large tendering lists which increase the cost of tendering which must eventually be passed on to the client. Probably the most common procedure is the invitation to a list of selected contractors known by the authority's technical officers to have the necessary experience and capacity. It can be argued that this leaves the authority open to the possibility of 'ring' tendering. Probably the most sophisticated, though much the least common, procedure is that of the serial tender. In this case contractors from a selected list can be invited to tender for a stated share of the authority's entire building programme on the basis of a prototype bill of quantities which requires the contractor to quote a rate for items of work most likely to occur within the proposed programme. This system can be particularly useful when the programme is based on the use of a building system. In this case objection may be raised on the ground that too small a group of large contractors may corner the market and that the liquidation of any serial contractor will have serious consequences. A further method adopted is to advertise each project in the technical and local press and to select a restricted list of tenderers from the response. This had the merit of ensuring that tenderers are keen to have the work, but requires detailed examination of the suitability of tenderers for each contract and is costly in time and advertising.

In short, tendering procedures vary; all of them have their critics; and by and large, authorities tend to favour one or the other rather than to 'dabble' in all. Experience seems to indicate that, at any rate where the system building from factory components is to be used, a high level of cost effectiveness is to be gained from the serial method. It should be noted that the National Joint Consultative Committee for Building (18 Mansfield Street, London, W1M 9FG) publishes recommended procedures for the various methods of tendering which is extremely helpful in establishing methods of operation which assist the client and are acceptable to the industry.

Tenders having been received, and the necessary DES procedures followed, the stage is set for the start on site. Every effort is then geared to meet the planned opening date. Here again, much of the work is left to the technical people—contractors, architects, quantity surveyors, building inspectors, and the staff of the public utilities. Staff at the Education Office still have a role to play, however. In some authorities there will be furniture and equipment to order, matching the time scales for delivery with the progress of the building work. In all authorities there is the need to monitor the rate of progress on the project in order to relate this to the timing for proposed staffing and to compare the expenditure to date with the budget figure for the current year. Above all, the Education Committee is still the client, and it is important that the educationist recognizes the responsibility that implies. Last minute hitches, sudden needs to agree minor changes and, in the case of extensions and rehabilitations to existing schools, the possible need to arbitrate between the staff of the school and the architect all require an awareness of the current state of the development without any active participation on site. Excellent relationships and good communication between the architect and the educationist continue to be vital to the success of the project.

Given reasonable weather, no unsuspected site problems, no industrial disputes to hold up supplies of materials or to impede the actual building process on site, as the completion date approaches what started out as piles of materials and seemingly unrelated trenches and holes takes on the shape of a school. Before the authority will accept the building from the contractor come the formalities of take-over inspections and the preparation of a schedule of agreed defects and deficiencies which will have to be put right. The 'builders' clean' is followed by the more comprehensive 'clean' by caretaking and cleaning staff. Portable furniture and equipment pour into the building.

In the case of a new school, it is usually about this stage that teaching staff begin to appear, and soon after (and often before the entire building is absolutely complete) the pupils arrive and a school is born.

If this brief and all too superficial survey concentrates attention on country primary and secondary schools and makes no reference to special school or further education building programmes; if it does not treat the special features of voluntary school building, it is only through lack of space. In general it may be said, however, that the principles which underlie the building and furnishing of voluntary schools, of special schools, of colleges of further education, are broadly the same as those which underlie the building of country primary and secondary schools. However, while the principles may be broadly the same, the complexity of the provision and the infrequency of major projects in further education demand of the administrator and architect a willingness to consult, learn and exercise humility which is even greater than it would be in more familiar projects.

A general point may perhaps be made. More than once in this survey attention has been directed to the role of the DES in the education building process. It is worthy of note that as far as school building controls are concerned, over the years since the Second World War the hand of central government has rested more and more gently on the guiding rein. Any anxiety which there could have been about the possibility of central standardization of school buildings should by now have evaporated. The controls of the Standards for Schools Premises Regulations, for instance, have become less detailed and, so far as the planning of individual projects has been concerned, decisions have been left to the local authorities. After all it was upon them that the 1944 Act imposed the duty 'to secure that there shall be available for all the area sufficient schools . . . sufficient in number, character and equipment to afford for all pupils opportunities for education offering such variety of instruction and training as may be desirable in view of their differing ages, abilities and aptitudes . . .' It is a duty which on the whole they have well discharged.

Why 'on the whole'? Like all things born, a new school needs support from the moment it comes into existence. It will age and, as it ages, will more and more need repair and maintenance. One would like to think that the design and specification of new school buildings kept firmly in mind ease and economy of future maintenance. But it is hard to escape the conclusion that financial constraints on capital expenditure cause us to neglect or even create future maintenance problems. In the attempt to make too little money go further than it effectively can we probably reached a stage some years ago where what we have built cheaply we shall maintain at great expense. Acres of leaking flat roofs will perhaps serve as one of the most readily recognized examples. And the problem is compounded by the frequency with which, in a period of restraint on revenue budgets, authority allocations for the maintenance of buildings have been squeezed until deterioration of the fabric of school buildings has reached a stage of galloping consumption.

There are those who hold that the rapid changes in teaching methods and the internal organization of schools demand that no schools should be designed to last for more than about 20 years. It is a view hardly likely to commend itself to elected members or to treasurers paying for building, as most of them are, over a period of 60 years.

Somewhat less obvious perhaps is the effect of neglected maintenance on the ambience of a school. It may, with some justice be claimed that the educational benefits which accrue from a stimulating, colourful decor and from tasteful furnishings are of immense importance. Particularly will this be so in schools serving areas of social deprivation where the school may well be the most attractive and welcoming environment in which a child finds himself. If this be true, it must follow that the neglect of maintenance represents an important reduction in the educational opportunity which a well-maintained building has to offer.

Arrangements for maintenance of buildings vary from authority to authority. In some cases all, or most, of the work is carried out by direct labour organizations; in others work is put out to private contractors. In almost every case the responsibility rests on the authority's chief architect or building services manager and the role of the educational administrator is sometimes seen as being limited to that of intermediary between school and architect—passing on requests for repairs, identifying buildings in special educational need or, as some architects would no doubt claim, complaining perpetually—complaining of declining standards, standards of resource allocation, standards of workmanship, standards of materials used. It should, however, be regarded as something more important, if the limited resources available for maintenance are to be used efficiently. Replacing like with like, for example, is not necessarily in the best interests of the present or future needs of the school and an educationist's knowledge of successful initiatives in one school may enable another to maximize the opportunity for change that some minor maintenance works present.

The development area is one which has always offered considerable challenges to the Education Officer and in this area, as in others, the changes in legislation will require skills of the highest order if needs and resources are to be used effectively. It is also true that it is a field of work which contains the potential for frustration to perhaps a greater degree than most. It will be evident from what has gone before that the rationalization of building stock is a highly sensitive operation and it is hardly surprising that elected members are most reluctant to be held responsible for closing schools, even when the financial state of the local authority as a whole may be less than healthy. The professional may find it more difficult to accept the crude abuse of the Capital programme for political ends. Just as the closure of a school may well lose a local politician some votes, the opening of a school is regarded as a very attractive option. If a logical order of priorities is to prevail, the Education Officer may have to work very hard indeed to commit his committee in advance to a structured programme with which it is difficult to tamper. If he is not successful in this endeavour, he may well have to face the steady infiltration of low priority projects into the high priority places as politicians carry out their endless manoeuvres for personal advantage.

Just as the order of major projects may be affected by a disregard for logical criteria, so too the officer may find himself under heavy pressure to reduce minor works allocations in order to create space for more new building. New buildings are attractive: a wide range of minor works adaptation is less visible to the public eye and does not so readily reflect to the glory of the particular local member.

The other major area of concern experienced by the Manager is the use of Public Works Departments to carry out maintenance work. Although recent legislation has forced Authorities to be more careful in their use of Direct Works organizations, the commitment of many local authorities to the principle of Direct Works may well work to the disadvantage of the Education service. It is not surprising that a clash frequently emerges between the Council's priorities for the Public Works Department which involve a year-long programme to maximize the use of its staff and other resources and the needs of the Education Department which ideally would prefer to control the services which it is offered. Few Education Officers will be unaware of the problems which are caused by the programming of work in schools at a time which is convenient to the Direct Works organization but highly inconvenient to the management of the schools. The most glaring example is that of painting programmes which, instead of being carried out during vacation, are undertaken during term time. Although many direct service organizations tend to deliver a good service, the disparity of interest between them and their clients is a fundamental weakness in that context, the lesser irritations relating to the control of information, accountancy procedures and methods of charging assume a greater potential for irritation. It will be interesting to see how great a role is played in decisions about the future states of schools by head teachers who have experienced years of subordination to the so-called support services operated by local authorities.

The main challenges for the Department of Education and Science and LEAs over the years to the end of the century will be five-fold—first, a constant monitoring and evaluation of building stock in each LEA area as set out in the 'Study of School Building' paper produced by the Department of

Education and Science in 1977; second, the remodelling of old schools and design of new schools to take account of new curriculum developments and interventions by such outside bodies as the Manpower Services Commission (MSC), and the wider community use of educational buildings; third, the furnishing and equipping of educational institutions; fourth, a closer examination of the design of and provision for Further Education (FE) colleges, etc; and finally, overriding all of these, the possible consequences of recent legislation for the rational use of an authority's building stock. Let us examine these challenges one by one.

1. Attempts to evaluate the school building stock must look both at the changes, past and future, that affect its adequacy; and at the economic context in which plans for future capital investment are made. This review must take into account (*a*) Substantial and continuing changes in educational policies, techniques and methods, in the role of the school in society, and in the attitudes and expectations of society itself; (*b*) educational developments such as the reorganization of schools on comprehensive lines, the reduction of class sizes, the extension of nursery education, the introduction of increasingly active methods of learning and the growing links between school and community all impose new demands on school buildings; and (*c*) changes in curriculum.

   In addition account must be taken of society's continually rising expectations for standards of safety, health and amenity of which the Health and Safety at Work etc. Act, 1974 is one example.
2. The remodelling of old schools and the design of new schools has to take account of the national curriculum, the introduction of some of the new technologies, the much wider community of use of schools and so on. In primary school built before the Second World War we have been left with a great number of the two or three decker variety (mainly in London and the cities) and of those whose single classrooms approached by long corridors radiate at different angles from the assembly

hall and administrative area. As rolls fall so spare cellular classrooms have been and are being used variously for library/resource centres, TV educational programmes, withdrawal groups of different kinds or just for storage. In some schools some classroom doors debouching on the corridors have been opened and apparatus, equipment, books and carpeting have spilt over into them; where a pair of teacher in adjacent classrooms have agreed to do this together for the same age group, co-operative teaching and (incidentally) in-service, on the job, training of these teachers begins to take place; the curriculum is enriched and widened and the problems of differing individual abilities approached much more effectively. This sort of experience needs to be explored in remodelling old primary schools, as does the wide experience of open-planning which has developed over the country as a whole in the last twenty years. Teaching methods do change, however, and the opportunity to remodel a school occurs very seldom. The design must therefore allow for flexibility of teaching styles, which may not necessarily reflect those of the teachers currently on the school staff.

Minor works projects to effect remodelling are probably the quickest method LEAs can employ, but care must be taken to ensure that any major maintenance works that have to be included are costed accurately, so that there is no risk that the cost of the capital works appears to exceed the minor works limit. Remodelling of old primary schools will need to take account of the increased use of microcomputers, with their need for mobility within the school and the associated security consequences as well as appropriate facilities for the under-fives and the relevant school building regulations for children of nursery age.

In secondary schools the introduction of the national curriculum, the continuing development of comprehensive education, the greater emphasis on technical and vocational education within the general education context and the greater use of new technology in the shape of microcomputers and other sophisticated equipment all point to the need to re-assess the distribution and use of practical areas. In remodelling schools, the administrator, architect and quantity surveyor, working in close collaboration with teachers and advisers, need to bear in mind changing attitudes to the curriculum and to reflect these in the new design. This is true not only of practical and laboratory areas, but also of provision for the arts—especially the performing arts such as music, dance and drama—and for physical education and recreation.

Remodelling secondary schools certainly should have regard to community use. More and more, certain secondary schools are being designated as community colleges or centres for the use of the whole community. In rural areas especially, and increasingly in urban neighbourhoods, selected primary schools are being designated as community focal points. In most of these cases, in addition to designing or modifying these buildings for community use, independent rooms like community common rooms with refreshment facilities and bars make them available when the rest of the building is in use for school purposes during the day. School rooms will be used increasingly by adults and will be so eve.. more especially if practical and other rooms have been designed with joint adult-school student use in mind.

In country areas, improved facilities over and above what can be provided within school building costs can be achieved by developing joint schemes with district councils. Swimming baths, squash and badminton courts, all-weather floodlit playing areas, even restaurants and exhibition areas have been provided by joint schemes planned well in advance along with an agreed school building project.

Although attractive possibilities for multiple use exist, two caveats must be entered. First, it will be necessary to take account of the inevitable consequences for building, maintenance and depreciation costs. In this connexion, there is often a failure to acknowledge that a school's budget will suffer considerably if its equipment, which is often designed to standards directly related to education functions for children are heavily used by adults. Second, the increased power given to governing bodies in recent years means that they have greater control over the use of their school's buildings by other users, which can make it more difficult for LEAs to rationalize the use of the buildings in a particular area.

3. The furnishing and equipping of schools and colleges need careful attention since school supplies are a major item of expenditure in the budget of an education authority. As they have grown in range, complexity and sophistication, so they have increased in price. Attempts over the years since the war to establish cost formulae for the furnishing and equipping of primary, secondary and FE establishments have all failed. Now the costs must be obtained from within the overall building allocation for the LEA. It is relatively easy to decide on a percentage of the capital cost of a primary school to devote to loose furniture, but much more difficult to do this with secondary schools or colleges of FE and Polytechnics. Efforts have been made in the field of school building to obtain better value for money through standardization and the establishment of building consortia. These were aimed at securing the financial advantages of large-scale manufacture and purchasing. In the field of equipment and supplies the story of recent years has been much the same. Many of the larger authorities, at any rate, have central purchasing machinery operating on behalf of all departments. Often this has been built up on the foundation of an education supplies department. At one stage further along the line, we find consortia of local authorities. Thus, for example, CLEAPSE (Consortium of Local Education Authorities for the Purchase of Scientific Equipment) consists of some 51 authorities who have joined together to test and purchase scientific equipment and to encourage design and development. The Countries Furniture Group (CFG)

has set up its own design team and all 47 authorities in full or associate membership can contribute through their officers and advisers. new prototypes and designs more sensitive to developing educational needs. Consequently there has been an overall aesthetic and ergonomic approach to furnishings which has gone some way to achieve an overall design and finish—something sadly lacking in the heterogeneous furniture to be seen in most older schools.

The furniture consortia followed in the footsteps of the big school building consortia like SCOLA and CLASP which were established in the early 1960s to cope with the rapid expansion of the school population and of the basic need of school building. Nevertheless much remains to be done between educators, architects and manufacturers before the furnishing of schools and colleges is carried out functionally and aesthetically in a really effective way.

Some individual authorities have moved towards standardization through the compilation of lists of approved teaching aids from which their schools must select when making purchases, particularly of expensive equipment. This is a step towards securing not only the benefits of bulk buying, but also the monitoring of the quality and suitability of equipment—a necessary precaution in a rapidly growing commercial market. Another common arrangement is the provision centrally by an authority of stocks of some kinds of equipment—records, cassettes, projectors and the like—which can be taken out on loan by schools. One may perhaps wonder how long this practice is likely to be justified given the increasing delicacy of some of the more sophisticated items and hence their vulnerability to damage during transit. The quite alarming costs of postage and transport also suggest that the advantages of such an arrangement are likely to be felt more immediately in urban authorities with large numbers of schools within a radius of a few miles even though central lending services were in some cases at any rate, originally conceived with the need of small and scattered rural schools in mind. Certainly it is in such places that the provision of central stocks of relatively small items has become uneconomic because of changes in the availability and cost of transport at a time when the cost of purchase of such equipment, in relative terms, has fallen and its reliability increased.

4. The design, planning and equipping of FE establishments present many problems of administration and management. Since the war, a vast building programme for AFE and NAFE has been undertaken. Recent legislation confirms the duty of each LEA to secure the provision of adequate further education to meet the needs of its area. FE colleges are now required to accept a greater responsibility for their financial affairs and to respond to the provision for free trade at a time when they are beginning to feel the effects of a drop in the age cohort and are being pressed by Central Government to provide additional management information and become more cost effective. Pressure for places in colleges is heavy and will probably be increasingly so due to demands from industry, from young people seeking additional qualifications to enhance their employability and from the programmes of MSC to which reference is made in another chapter. Financial and other resources for building and the up-dating and replacement of technical equipment are likely to be limited, and therefore very careful management and assessment of demand by administrators, college principals and other staff will be necessary if the response is to be adequate.
5. The effects of the 1988 Act have yet to be fully felt. The impact of the removal from local authority control of polytechnics and some colleges of higher education is likely to be felt more in the colleges themselves than by the authorities. By contrast, the Act takes a stage further the process of moving responsibility for the running of institutions from the local authorities to the schools and colleges of further education.

Three sets of provisions may be cited to illustrate how the 1988 legislation offers the possibility of the disruption of arrangements for planning and delivering of the programme for managing the plant and resources of the Authority, viz., those which relate to City Technology Colleges, grant-maintained schools, and admission limits, respectively. City Technology Colleges if successful will attract considerable numbers of students who would otherwise have been accommodated in maintained secondary schools. At a time when falling rolls have put the viability of many schools in the balance, the additional, though marginal, drain on the pool of potential students could have a critical effect. The movement of schools to grant-maintained status combines the possibility of losing students with that of loss of school plant by the LEA. This could cause the Authority to reconsider its overall provision and detailed arrangements. Within a three-tier system, involving first, middle and high schools, the impact could be particularly severe, especially in authorities which have developed closely integrated pyramid organizations.

The change in the regulations governing admission limits of itself threatens the stability of declining schools. The additional challenge of grant-maintained schools potentially exacerbates an already difficult situation. To maintain stability and economically effective provision of plant and resources will be administratively more intricate as the new admission procedures and limits come into force.

Taken together, the three provisions adumbrated above offer the possibility of an improvement for a minority at the expense of disruption of the planning processes designed to bring benefits to the greatest number. It will not be a simple matter for an authority to prevent a narrowing of opportunity for those students in LEA maintained institutions affected by the impact of grant-maintained schools and City Technology Colleges, nor to support schools in particular localities which are already vulnerable to one form or another of drift.

Provisions for local financial management and their interaction with the legislation in the Local Government Act for competitive tendering will significantly affect the role of the Education Officer. Schemes for local financial management are to be prepared for September 1989, for full implementation by 1993. Capital provision for schools is excluded from the arrangements, but expenditure on maintenance will become a dual responsibility. The Secretary of State expects local authorities to delegate responsibility to schools for non-structural maintenance such as painting and the repair of broken windows and doors, while retaining responsibility for structural maintenance. Similarly, schools should have delegated powers in respect of ground maintenance but the Authority should purchase capital items such as tractors. While the general landlord-tenant relationship is offered as a guide within which to develop a scheme, many issues will inevitably arise which will not be simple to resolve.

The devolution of financial management to individual institutions will diminish the flexibility which the LEA has hitherto enjoyed to meet contingencies and crises in the maintenance of the total educational plant. As its role becomes more strategic exercising oversight over schools and colleges managing their own maintenance, LEAs will need to devise procedures to protect institutions against emergencies, inflation and unusual occurrences.

The 1988 Act and associated notes of guidance make clear Government's intention to give schools within schemes of local financial management the opportunity to enjoy as much freedom as possible to choose the means and nature of delivery of services which at present are provided by local authorities. The implications for direct service organization concerned with building, grounds maintenance, vehicle maintenance, cleaning and catering are intriguing. The reactions of governing bodies to this offer of freedom will be affected by a range of factors: political beliefs, previous experience of local authority services, consideration of potential economies. Similar considerations will apply to consortia which have developed to purchase and deliver school equipment and furniture on a regional basis and beyond. The entire philosophy and practice of local authorities which see themselves as contractors is likely to be modified.

All these changes are going to make it increasingly difficult for local authorities to plan resources and plant in a reliable nd effective way. The challenge for the department of Education and Science will be no less. The relationship of competing demands from grant maintained schools, city technology colleges, independent HE establishments as well as from the LEAs will undoubtedly make it even more difficult for the Department's officers to determine priorities.

In conclusion it will be appreciated from reading this chapter that the actual management of educational plant is becoming more complex and will challenge Education and Architects' Departments of LEAs on a scale perhaps unforeseen in the years since the war. At present the opportunity exists, mainly through minor works, to remodel schools and colleges on a modest scale to keep pace with curriculum change, with the wider community use of schools (especially secondary schools), with the introduction of new technologies, and with the wider responsibilities laid on LEAs for example, with regard to the special educational needs and multi-cultural education. The need for Education Departments to develop long term strategies for remodelling work, at least to the end of the century, will remain and indeed become more important. Certainly, in the light of recent legislation, increases in parental choice and governors' responsibilities and the possibilities of opting out will become administratively more demanding.

9

Financing of Schools

INTRODUCTION

Some educators gain the impression that the major limitation on educational development is finance. Some who work outside the service believe that he who pays the piper should call the tune. No longer is there a majority view that increasing financial provision for education will lead to a solution of most of the country's problems. On the contrary, there are those who are critical of the nature and costs of some aspects of the education service and seek to absolve themselves from the responsibility of solving problems by blaming education for causing those problems. It is not surprising, therefore, that the costs as well as the aims and processes of education are looked at by more people and much more critically than formerly and that general financial controls now appear to be more numerous and applied with a tighter rein. Paradoxically, however, a greater freedom of choice within limited budgets has developed in a number of areas—the choices open to head teachers, for example. Education is similar to most activities in that finance can be used either as a carrot or a stick. One of the difficulties experienced by an educational administrator is that, to many others, it seems superficially so easy to apply the stick by a small percentage reduction in expenditure or, less frequently, to provide a small percentage carrot.

Figures about expenditure usually convey little information other than their size. Until 1981 Government expenditure plans were detailed at constant prices and it was possible, for example, to calculate the changing cost per pupil over about a ten-years period including the proposed cost for a three-year planned period. Even these figures could not indicate how far falling rolls, curricular changes, national economic problems, changing attitudes to expenditure on education or, in secondary education, the increased proportion of older pupils contributed to the changes in unit costs.

In 1982 the Government switched their financial planning to cash terms, making it even more difficult to make sensible assessments of the likely volume, or indeed quality of services which may be provided.

The most helpful publication on unit costs with calculations relating to actual costs for two years is the annual Handbook of Education Unit Costs prepared by the Financial Information Unit of the DES and published by CIPFA. Also published by CIPFA are annual statistics of estimated unit costs based upon LEAs' budgets for the year ahead.

The decade from 1979 was marked by constant debate about local government finance in general and education finance in particular. The culmination was legislation in 1988 introducing the community charge to replace the domestic rates, requiring competition in certain services, and setting a new statutory framework for the financial management of schools and colleges. More than ever before the administrator needs to devote time and effort to explain the real relationship between finance and service to those who, such as the teachers, spend the money and provide the service and those, such as the elected members and the public, who provide the money. The educational administrator will realize, however, teacher that he is, that no teacher can teach well anything that he does not himself fully understand. Even if he would prefer to spend most of his time thinking and talking about education, he must of necessity learn and then talk about its finance.

EXPENDITURE

Control

Central government needs to be able to have a reasonable measure of influence on, some would say control of, expenditure in the local authority education service, which accounts for over 80 per cent of all public expenditure on education, science and arts. The LEA must control education expenditure which, in some areas, is more than two-thirds of its total expenditure. However such controls have to be reconciled with the inescapable reality that a teacher must be able to spend money on books, a college head of department on new equipment, a careers officer on a careers exhibition, a youth leader on club heating, or an educational administrator on teachers' salaries or on equipping a new school.

Education expenditure, like all local government expenditure, is authorized by statute or orders and regulations made by Ministers. Such authorization does not imply uniformity. The first major enquiry into local government finance for 60 years, often referred to as the Layfield Report, in 1976 noted that it is difficult to find elements in the education service that are not open to local variation in interpretation of the statutory requirements—that it is difficult to distinguish between functions which are mandatory on the authority and those which are discretionary. The legal duty 'to secure efficient education to meet the needs of the population' is an example of a duty imposed commonly on all LEAs but whose cost cannot commonly be measured. On the other hand, the cost of mandatory student awards can be readily assessed.

Government Decision and Advice

The often heard description of education as a national service locally administered leads to the expectation—which is fulfilled—that a considerable proportion of education expenditure is determined by central government. The national prescription of the standards for school buildings is a good example of minimum provision determined centrally, leaving limited local discretion about the actual levels and costs of provision. In addition to making statutes and regulations, government issues circulars which often give advice about levels of service and, partly because of the consultations with local authority associations which normally precede the issue of circulars, advice is treated seriously, although local circumstances, particularly financial limitations, may lead authorities to respond only slowly. Salaries of teachers account for more than half the expenditure of LEAs. The scales of salaries for teachers are unusual in that they are imposed on LEAs by a statutory instrument, so that a very substantial part of an authority's expenditure is to some extent centrally determined.

In 1980 the Government developed a new assessment of expenditure needs usually referred to as GREs (Grant Related Expenditures). The system was intended to be more comprehensible, stable and equitable, encompassing plausible and intelligible factors, excluding so far as possible differences which are the result of local preferences. GREs were said to be an attempt to measure the cost of a common level of service and as such were given a cautious welcome. It soon became clear, however, that the appropriate common level of service was not the prime consideration. It was the fact that the costs in aggregate were to be consistent with the Government's expenditure plans for the year that determined the 'acceptable' level of service. Moreover, the arguments about weighting to be given to the different parts of a service and to the factors affecting the costs of providing a given level of service have continued. What weighting should be given to special needs, and how should the various contributory factors be calculated, for example? Or how should sparsity of population be related to educational costs? Nevertheless, for the first time attempts were made to calculate the cost of providing some level of service and undoubtedly the assessments will improve. Government calculations of GREs for individual services may have considerable influence on actual expenditure on those services in spite of the apparent wish of many who are not concerned with specific services to concentrate on general grants and freedom of local authorities to spend as they wish. A detailed example is that in 1987 and 1988 DES gave indicative allocations to each authority of new 'A' incentive allowances for teachers' salaries based on factors used in the calculation of GREs. The full significance may become apparent as central government assumes greater control of local government finance generally following the introduction of the community charge when it will be more difficult for authorities to depart from expenditure norms by raising taxes locally.

Assumptions about the maintenance or change of education policies are built into the government's annual announcements about local government finance. However, after the statutory orders have been laid before Parliament to implement the government decisions, the subsequent circular from central government to local authorities invariably contains an observation that the decisions on expenditure on individual services are properly a matter for each local authority. The decisions of authorities vary. Some try to match, as far as possible, percentage changes in government estimates to their own situations, bearing in mind demographic and other factors. Others, particularly those that either receive considerable benefits or suffer disadvantages from changes in the distribution of grant or calculations of GRE or financial targets may well be much more generous or much tougher than government guidelines suggest. In practice, however, government guidelines have always had a considerable influence on most authorities. The influence is not always one way, however. In 1986 government expenditure plans for education for 1987/88 had to be adjusted upwards by over £2 billion to bring them closer to the cumulative total of expenditure by all LEAs. The collective view of the LEAs was that the needs of the service were greater than those implied by government assumptions. Using the freedom to raise taxes (the rates) locally enabled the needs to be met.

The development of the Training Commission has had a very considerable effect on the financing of non-advanced further education. Although not directly part of central government the large central government funds the Commission distributes are in effect seen as specific grants often with linked expenditure controls.

Government action to contain general levels of local government expenditure has an effect on local decisions about education spending. The establishment of the Audit Commission in 1982 has resulted in a number of influential reports on economy, efficiency and effectiveness in specific service areas; the statutory power to 'cap' an authority's level of community charge can effectively limit absolutely the capacity of the authority to spend in a given year; the requirement for competition in services such as meals, cleaning, grounds and vehicle maintenance ensures that expenditure levels are comparable with the private sector.

Inter-authority Agreements

A second group of expenditure determinants involves part of the education service where LEAs believe it to be either to their advantage and/or fair to individuals to have nationally accepted standards. LEAs work through either the Association of Country Councils (ACC) for non-metropolitan authorities or the Association of Metropolitan Authorities (AMA) or jointly through the Council of Local Education Authorities (CLEA). These organizations negotiate with the DES, teachers' associations and others to produce recommended expenditure policies. Examples are recoupment payments to be made by LEAs to each other for educating one another's pupils or students, some conditions of service, and levels of payment for residential duties in special schools (which seem to be generally accepted by LEAs) and the levels of fees for non-advanced full-time further education courses and grants for discretionary awards (which are not always accepted). The recommendations of the associations are usually adopted by LEAs and expenditure patterns are consequently predetermined in certain areas.

LEA Financial Planning

Each LEA has its own rule book on finance—often referred to as Financial Regulations—to deal with the mechanics of financial transactions and to ensure the proper safeguarding of public money. The major control exercised by the local authority is its annual approval of estimates of expenditure. Just as no Council can make a decision on an educational matter without a report from its Education Committee (unless, in their opinion, the matter is urgent), equally no financial commitment can be entered into by the Education Committee or its officers except within the limits of estimates approved by the Council. Only the Council can set the level of the community charge or borrow money. As far as revenue expenditure is concerned the final approval is normally given by annually approved estimates. In most authorities capital expenditure is similarly approved annually. Some authorities have additions—rolling programmes of expenditure, for example—or requirements that certain items of expenditure —of a particular type or above a given level—should receive specific council approval. Whatever the local arrangements may be, the authority to incur expenditure is given ultimately by the Council and the annual review of expenditure and income is usually the focus of the LEA's financial activities.

Some policy changes may have little financial effect but others may have considerably more, especially in the medium and longer terms. For example, a reorganization of secondary education throughout an authority's area may require a multi-million pound building programme and a well-thought-out plan to provide adequate in-service training for teachers over a number of years. Such changes require long-term financial commitments which constitute inescapable expenditure spread over a number of years. Variations in the levels of annual expenditure cannot be allowed to prejudice such commitments.

The cumulative effect of commitments arising from central government statutory or advisory powers, from local authority and governors' duties, policies and agreements, and from continuing consequences of local policy decisions, is such that a large part of education expenditure is virtually fixed and not subject to variation. The consequences of relatively rapid changes in income—as from government grants—or in expenditure—such as inflation—can be very severe on the few remaining areas of expenditure which can be made subject to rapid change, such as provision of books or discretionary grants.

Assessing Local Needs

The needs of individual children, of students, of the community vary widely. If it is accepted, as it should be by Education Officers, that the education service exists to satisfy, or to help to satisfy, those needs, then the assessment of those needs and discussion about the methods of satisfying, or helping to satisfy them, is required before there can be any realistic decisions about the education budget. In determining institutional needs general formulae statistically derived from practice and experience may be used to give guidance on teaching and non-teaching staffing levels and on expenditure on items such as books, equipment and out-of-school activities. Assumptions about the spending needs of institutions in a variety of different circumstances must inform the total assessment of the expenditure required. Schools that are remote or with many immigrants or with particular problem children who are deprived, physically or mentally, are obvious variants from the average, as is the college with a high proportion of craft students or the youth club in the difficult inner-city area. It may be equally important, however, to give some special help to the establishment which has just lost a senior member of staff who has allowed some aspect of work to run down. Attention has to be given to staff development, to helping teachers and others the better to reflect changes in knowledge, methods and teaching, the internal organization of the school, the community in which they live or the national or international scene.

All the above have to be considered before arriving at the total expenditure requirements of each sector of the service, nursery education, primary and secondary education, further education and so on. For schools and for colleges individual budget shares will be determined by a formula, largely pupil or student number driven, approved by the Secretary of State. The formula must be designed to meet as great a variety of local circumstances as possible. Critical decisions have to be taken about funds to be held centrally which may be no more than 10 per cent of the total for schools or 15 per cent for colleges.

Consultation

Discussions about institutional needs will be interwoven with proposals for change, either from central government or from the local authority. Education Officers and advisers will meet groups of employees. Discussions with staff representatives, particularly through the union representatives, may take place. The introduction of formula funding for schools and colleges following the Education Reform Act, 1988 requires extensive and regular consultation with governing bodies. In cases of major change and annual consideration of financial priorities, elected members may be involved.

Consultation with governors of a school or college or with members of the local community may prompt or reveal possible voluntary action which can help to solve local problems or create new opportunities, the financial consequences of which need careful consideration. In particular, there will be discussions with governors of aided schools who have certain financial responsibilities for the care of the school fabric and with organizations and committees concerned with activities which the authority supports financially or operates jointly. By no means all the actions which are essential or desirable for any institution or any community will have financial implications, although in practice a high proportion do, and these implications are not necessarily obvious in the early stages of formulations of proposals.

It is inevitable that a good deal of consultation with governors, head teachers and principals will be concerned with the effectiveness of the authority's formula for calculating the budget share for individual schools and colleges and taking full account of the particular needs of the pupils or students involved. Similarly discussions have to take place about the performance indicators to be used to show the efficiency and effectiveness of the spending decisions by governors in relation to the education of the pupils and students for whom they are responsible. To be complete, measures of performance not only have to show that the accounts properly balance but need to address measures of educational output. This is a notoriously difficult task requiring some assessment of the external factors affecting educational performance such as home and school environment.

Consultation with governors on the budget formula also extends to the services to be required from the authority. For example, will the governors be making their own arrangements for cleaning the school, or will they be using the service offered by the authority, whether 'in-house' or through a private contractor?

Consultation about capital expenditure normally takes place in the same way. Building programmes and consequent site and equipment requirements are dealt with in a separate chapter. In addition, however, initial and replacement provision of vehicles—buses or delivery vans, for example—the provision of large items of equipment for new further and higher education courses, capital grants to voluntary organizations, and, in some authorities, replacement of equipment, must receive regular consideration. The decision about whether to finance such expenditure from revenue or loan is not a matter for the Education Committee or the Education Officer.

Discussions about expenditure are normally limited to groups who are particularly concerned. For example, the money needed by the careers service in helping to deal with the unemployed is not likely to be discussed with primary school representatives, a variation of the budget formula to provide more weighting for ancillary help for the under-fives will not be on the agenda for the further education teacher discussions, and the discretionary element of the Salaries Document will not interest the youth leaders or psychologists. The Education Officer is, however, concerned with the whole of the education service. Sufficient finance will never be available to do all that is put forward from separate institutions or from particular groups of employees. The Education Officer must weigh up the merits of the proposals and the financial, as well as political practicalities and investigate alternative ways of satisfying needs.

He will at various stages discuss proposals with colleagues in other relevant departments as well as with the chairman and, probably, some senior members of the Education Committee. When some order of priorities between all the claims of the education service has been decided by the

Education Committee it will be either the chairman of the committee briefed by the officer or the officer himself who will argue the case for education expenditure in competition with expenditure on other services—social services, roads, fire service, for example—or with those who would prefer reductions in expenditure.

Education Expenditure

The references so far have been to matters which are, without doubt, educational. Maintenance of buildings in which education takes place will probably be accepted as an educational expense. Maintenance of pupils or students is more doubtful.

School meals are sometimes a matter of dispute. No longer does the government fix the charge per meal. Precise nutritional and staffing levels are not prescribed nationally, as was once the case. The 1980 Education Act limited the duty of authorities for the provision of a mid-day meal just to children from families in financial need, and the Social Security Act, 1986 limited the power to provide free meals only to children from families qualifying for 'Family Support'. For other pupils there is a power (exercised by most, but not all authorities) to provide a mid-day meal at a charge for those who bring sandwiches. There are wide variations in local authorities' charging practices and, partly in consequence, in net school meals expenditure. It is generally, but not universally, accepted that the broad oversight of the school meals service, linked as it is with many other pupils' activities at mid-day and on the school site, is properly part of the responsibility of the head teacher. Nevertheless, the provision of mid-day meals and the way in which they are financed can be regarded as a welfare, not educational, matter and the inclusion of school meals expenditure under the 'education' heading is not regarded, by some, as appropriate. Following the Education Reform Act, 1988 schemes of financial delegation may provide for school meals expenditure to become the responsibility of school governors, thus allowing some decisions about 'education' and welfare priorities for expenditure to be made at school level.

The second largest item in many LEAs that may be regarded as non-educational expenditure, but one which can be very large in rural areas, is transport of pupils to school. Central government determines the distances above which pupils must be transported free to school. Authorities may have general lower limits and they may allow free transport in special cases, but increasingly they are having to provide free transport where there are considerations of road safety. There have been many long and detailed arguments for changes in the law and proposal to increase the LEAs' discretion but there has been no agreed conclusion. In 1980 the Government attempted to change the law to give LEAs more discretion over this expenditure but the proposal was defeated in the House of Lords.

Clothing and maintenance allowances to help children of poorer parents to benefit from education without hardship have a caring or welfare element and are not simply educational payments when paid in respect of children who are legally compelled to go to school. The justification for maintenance payments after the age of compulsory education, however, is largely educational. The introduction of the Government's Youth Training Scheme with attendant £25 per week training allowance and the variety of other payments available to those outside the education service illustrates the point well. It has been asserted that young people are being attracted away from school or college because they are financially better off unemployed or undergoing some form of education or training under YTS. Moreover the proportion of children of poorer parents still receiving full-time education after the compulsory school age limit is well below the levels for children of other parents. The main argument for education maintenance allowances is based on the need to encourage, and to avoid discouraging, full-time education. However, shortage of money seems to prevent some LEAs from increasing either the number or value of such awards.

In practice, until the late 1970s, it seemed to matter little that payments which were not narrowly and exclusively educational, and in some cases largely, if not wholly, welfare payments were met out of education budgets. However, it became very important for some LEAs when overall cost limits were applied. Decisions on the availability of finance for education in those LEAs depended to some extent on the finance required for school meals, transport, maintenance allowances and other such payments.

Delegation of Powers to Spend

The practices of local authorities in authorizing expenditure vary considerably. Once the revenue estimates are approved the authorization to spend within those estimates is normally delegated to the service committee and, through them, to sub-committees and some virement between headings of estimates is common. Considerable delegation to Officers and other staff is normal. Indeed, without substantial delegation services could not function effectively. There may be some items reserved to the Council or to the main committee, although generally these are large items, often of capital expenditure or directly linked to major policy changes.

In the education service there was for many years considerable debate and variety of practice about the delegation of spending powers to individual governing bodies or heads of institutions. The scheme introduced into Hertfordshire in the early 1950s, which gave the head of each educational establishment a bank account into which was paid a general allowance to cover most items of non-staff expenditure and from which the head paid his own bills, did not spread. At the time that the Hertfordshire scheme was introduced authorities generally restricted expenditure rigorously to expenditure headings. Gradually, however, it was recognized that virement between headings of estimates was likely to lead to more sensible expenditure, and delegation of authority to spend increased the levels of accountability of individuals for the service provided, rather than for the money spent. Delegation of freedom in staffing matters was slow to develop and in some areas was reversed for non-teaching staff following local government reorganization in 1974 and an upsurge in those areas of a confusion between corporate management and detailed central control.

The Education Reform Act, 1988 has introduced a statutory requirement for financial and staffing delegation to governing bodies of colleges, secondary schools, and primary schools with 200 or more pupils on roll. When fully implemented the legislation provides for the budget share for all schools and institutions subject to delegation to have power to spend the budget share according to their priorities, subject to advice from the Head or Principal.

The government's aims for delegation to schools say that effective schemes of delegation will:

(*a*) enable governing bodies and head teachers of schools to plan their use of resources to maximum effect in accordance with their own needs and priorities and
(*b*) make schools more responsive to their clients—parents, pupils, the local community and employers.

For the Education Officer, widespread delegation of spending powers to governing bodies means concentration on strategic issues of planning the total budget, monitoring performance, and advising governing bodies and heads of institutions. He is central to the authority's responsibilities for deciding the scope of delegation, establishing the formula for resource allocation, and setting out the conditions and requirements within which governing bodies must operate. The formal operation of sanctions may be rare, but monitoring and advice are essential to achieving the best educational value for money, and avoiding the damaging experience for pupils that would occur if matters had become so bad as to warrant invoking the power to withdraw delegation.

INCOME

The income to a local authority from which education expenditure is met comes from:

1. A general grant from central government towards the cost of services for which that authority is responsible (known as the Revenue Support Grant, or RSG for short).
2. Specific grants to cover the whole or part of the cost of selected activities.

3. The income from the commercial and industrial rate as determined nationally by central government (known as the National Non-Domestic Rate).
4. Fees, rents and other charges for services rendered to individuals or organizations, and, apart from a few minor items of income, from sources such as endowments.
5. The balance, from other sources of revenue of the local authority, largely the income from the community charge.

Revenue Support Grant

RSG (Rate Support Grant prior to 1990) is by far the most complicated of the five sources of income. Each year discussions take place between representatives of the local authority associations and central government. For the education service the main discussions take place between officers in the Expenditure Steering Group (Education) known as ESGE. These are followed by discussions for all local government services (including Education), firstly at officer level, and then between elected members in the Consultative Council on Local Government Finance. After discussing the levels of service, the size of government grant and its method of distribution, central government announces its conclusions about the level of relevant expenditure considered appropriate, the proportion which it is prepared to finance, and the method to be used to distribute the grant to local authorities.

The level of grants has varied considerably over the years. From 1980/81 when it was at 61 per cent of relevant expenditure there was a rapid reduction until 1988/89 when it stood at 46 per cent.

The methods of distribution, although intended to be based on an authority's needs on the one hand and resources on the other, have varied considerably and have caused considerable argument and, often, acrimony. On the one hand, counties have argued that their problems, often including increasing population and small, remote villages, require an increasing proportion of finance. On the other, metropolitan districts have argued that their problems, often involving declining populations and inner city problems, require a greater financial allocation. Reference is made to the introduction of Grant Related Expenditure (GRE) assessments as the basis for grant distribution earlier in the chapter.

After the government has decided on the total grant it will give to local authorities certain deductions are made before the distribution is effected. These deductions are mainly non-educational involving, for example, police and transport. One deduction is however, very much concerned with education. This is the amount which allows the government, after consultation with the local authority associations, to defray expenditure on the provision of services for local authorities and deduct the amount so spent from the total of the grants otherwise payable to local authorities. Those who seek the maximum autonomy for each local authority argue that no deductions should be made before grant is distributed. Each authority should be free to contribute, if it so wishes, to a particular organization. Others argue that there are certain educational needs which local authorities cannot meet individually and that if LEAs jointly do not make, or help to make, such provision then central government would do so, thus upsetting the balance of power that would follow any increase in the proportion of finance contributed to by central government.

In 1978 this facility was used by agreement to continue to fund, or partly fund:

The Schools Curriculum Development Council (equally with the DES)
The National Federation for Educational Research
The National Institute for Adult and Continuing Education and
The Further Education Staff College.

Changes in the list may be made from time to time, but with the central government responsibilities for the National Curriculum, and Schools Examination and Assessment Councils introduced in the Education Reform Act, 1988 a major area of activity which in the past was funded by local government using this mechanism may finally have been eliminated.

Specific Grants

At one time the whole education service was subject to a percentage grant and the school meals service to a 100 per cent grant. From 1958, however, various forms of block grant were introduced and local government argued strongly against most forms of specific funding. Nevertheless, some special grants applied, notably 75 per cent grant under Section 11 of the Local Government Act, 1966 designed to meet the needs of ethnic minorities from 'new commonwealth' areas, 100 per cent funding for prison education, and 90 per cent (subsequently 100 per cent) grant for expenditure on mandatory awards. Additional careers officer posts to help with the effects of unemployment were funded 100 per cent by the Department of the Employment. A constant cry from successive Secretaries of State has been that they have had no power to spend any money directly on the education service and that any government decision that development is needed is frustrated by the Block Grant System which allows only for additions to the general grant, which can then be spent—or not spent—by LEAs as they wish. Agreement by government and the local authority associations about an education priority cannot ensure that additional grant, provided by additions to relevant expenditure, is spent on that priority—or even on the education service.

It can be argued that education is a national service, that it is unfair to provide widely different opportunities within one nation and that central government should be able to finance, or provide inducements to LEAs to finance, what it believes to be necessary improvements. The need to avoid detailed central direction of the education service, and the consequent political danger, can also be argued whilst asserting the reasonableness of people, the influence of the ballot box locally to ensure adequate services, and a willingness to try to respond to reasonable proposals from central government. At a time of increasing resources few seem to wish to see direct government funding with a possible consequent increase of central control.

When resources are limited or reducing, the attraction of direct funding is much greater.

In 1977, for example, the Secretary of State talked about, but did not achieve, a specific grant to improve the quality of the education service by increasing the level of spending on in-service education for teachers. By 1984 the Government had introduced percentage grants for certain kinds of in-service training (subsequently to become the LEA Training Grant Scheme) and had funded a major curriculum project—the Technical and Vocational Education Initiative—by specific funding through the Manpower Services Commission. The Education (Grants and Awards) Act, 1984 took the process a step further by empowering the Secretary of State to fund specific projects through Education Support Grants, limited initially to $\frac{1}{2}$ per cent, and subsequently one per cent of total education expenditure. The Local Authority Associations argued that this could be the thin edge of the wedge that could eventually lead to a national system of education and that local government autonomy was being undermined. Others argued that what was being proposed was very little different from what was happening already, and to a much larger extent, by the way of Manpower Services Commission funded activities and that possibly the availability of specific grant powers at an earlier date could have had the effect of retaining within the DES and the local government service the training initiatives and developments which the MSC had undertaken.

By 1988 specific grants for the training of teachers and Education Support Grants were well established as an effective means of influencing LEAs in the introduction of government policies. While the Local Authority Associations are consulted annually about priorities for LEATGS and ESGs the agenda is set and finally decided by central government. Specific grants had been used to improve science and maths teaching, to introduce new technology, for the implementation of new mid-day supervision arrangements, and for the change to GCSE examinations. Some old grants were withdrawn to release central finance for grants for the introduction of the Education Reform Act, and local government had of course to pay for those activities no longer subject to grant but which had to be continued.

Not all specific grants come direct from central government. Reference has already been made to Training Commission funding, notably for the extension of TVEI, and for NAFE, but also for a variety of smaller projects. The Education Reform Act has introduced new arrangements for funding higher education courses in LEA colleges requiring specific grant negotiated with the Polytechnics and Colleges Funding Council. A significant number of LEAs have secured grant from the European Social Fund for vocational training courses.

The Education Officer has had to develop new skills of bidding for grant, monitoring performance, and accounting to funding bodies for the outcome.

A new, reverse form of specific grant was introduced in the 1988 Education Reform Act. The governors of any maintained primary or secondary school with more than 300 pupils may apply for Grant Maintained status, and if successful the school becomes independent of the LEA and directly funded by DES. Government recoup the cost of the school from the LEA the amount being determined annually according to the LEA's funding formula and an allowance for overheads.

The National Non-domestic Rate

Until 1990 over half the income to local government came from the local rate levied on domestic and on commercial and industrial property in the area. The same basic rate was applied to all main categories of property, but there was a system of rate relief for domestic ratepayers. Government had argued for many years that the rating system was unfair. The same household had to pay the same charge whether occupied by one or two or three or four people; many local government voters did not pay rates at all; industry and commerce had to pay substantial charges without significant influence in local elections. The Local Government Finance Act, 1988 introduced the community charge to replace domestic rates, and effectively nationalized the commercial and industrial rates by providing for a uniform national rate set initially by central government and adjusted annually for inflation. Transitional arrangements are needed initially to smooth the introduction of a single rate instead of the wide local variations which applied with local discretion. The new system restricts the freedom of authorities to raise revenue and substantially increases the proportion of local authority income subject to central control, from 46 per cent to about 75 per cent.

Charges

Most aspects of school education must be free and charges cannot be applied. The Education Reform Act, 1988 re-stated this general principle, distinguishing between school activities which in general (apart from individual music tuition) cannot be subject to charge, and out-of-school activities for which charges may be applied. Such charges which do apply generally cover the cost of the activity and are dealt with at school level rather than appearing as part of the formal income of the authority. The major exception is the charge for school meals. A feature of the financial difficulties of the 1970s and 1980s has been an increasing dependence of many schools on voluntary fund raising to enhance the resources provided by the authority. Some have argued that this is unfair on schools that may not have access to large sums of voluntary money in their locality, and that anyway central and local government should be required to provide the full cost of the needs of the schools and not just a basic minimum. Government, however, have encouraged local voluntary effort, and indeed continued Education Support Grant funding for information technology in schools had been made conditional on LEAs and schools raising voluntary funds from local industry.

Fees, rents and charges for services rendered to individuals and organizations can vary greatly from authority to authority although, for some services, fees may be standardized. The average costs of tuition for pupils of differing ages and for students in further education are calculated and agreed nationally and used by LEAs in paying for those from their area who are educated by other LEAs. Tuition fees for full-time advanced further education courses are determined by the Secretary of State and for full-time non-advanced and part-time vocational courses are recommended by regional or national groupings of local authorities. Most agreements with industry training boards and the representatives of the Training

Commission were based on the LEA taking responsibility for the education of those of 18 years of age and under (for whom the LEAs did not usually charge fees); and the employer accepting responsibility for the fees for the over-18s and for any training undertaken by the LEA for those under 18. This was a compromise between those who argue that employers should be responsible for all costs to LEAs for the education and training of their employees and the others who believe that, because employers pay rates, they should not be required to pay fees. However, following the introduction of the Youth Training Scheme in 1983, which included considerable lump sum payments by the Training Commission to employers or managing agents in respect of each trainee, new arrangements were negotiated by the Local Authority Associations with employers and standard charges for trainees were recommended.

Non-vocational classes have been generally recognized as a good leisure time activity but even more, as a contribution to an individuals's personal well-being and development. Attitudes of the LEAs towards the financing of these classes as educationally and socially worthwhile did not normally differ greatly. As resources became more limited in the 1970s and later, local authorities slowly developed divergent attitudes, some working towards making non-vocational fees lower and others increasing charges from nominal levels. By the late 1970s some authorities had made non-vocational courses almost self-supporting, although in other areas these courses continued to be heavily subsidized.

The income from charges and fees which are not laid down nationally or regionally is only a small proportion of LEA income. It is nevertheless useful for an LEA to be able to decide, for example, whether or not to subsidize local clubs or individuals. The amounts involved in so doing are small but the free or cheap use of accommodation for a youth club can make all the difference to a club's success or even survival. 'Pump priming' in the form of revenue, and sometimes capital, grants or subsidized charges to voluntary organizations usually leads to input by others of time and money which have many times the value of the LEAs help.

Community Charge

After all the estimated income from the above sources is totalled and set against the estimated cost of providing the services for which the LEA is responsible, together with a reserve to meet unforeseen requirements, there remains an anticipated excess of expenditure over income. This difference may be found in part from balances, *i.e.* the estimated difference between income and expenditure in the previous year. A further contribution to filling the gap may come from relatively small sources of income such as trusts and endowments, but the main contribution will be the community charge levied on the adult population of the area (with a few very limited exceptions). It is the duty of local authority to determine the level of the charge required to enable it to meet its financial obligations. In deciding on those obligations the authority will take into account not only the needs of its services, but the political judgement of the level of charge that its electors are willing to pay, and any limit on the community charge imposed by central government using powers first introduced in 1984.

CONCLUSION

This is not the place to discuss the merits of different methods of local government finance, either those which operated in the past or those considered for the future. The Layfield Report, Local Government Finance (Cmd 6453), issued in 1976, was the most thorough enquiry into local government finance for many years, but in spite of the committee's recommendations, no consensus of opinion in favour of major change was forthcoming. Finally, after twelve years of debate and a host of detailed changes to the Rate Support Grant system the government succeeded in passing legislation in 1988 to make the fundamental change introducing the new community charge. Whatever the merits, there is no doubt that the technicalities of the new system will be at least as great, and that financial knowledge and skills on the part of the Education Officer will be just as much at a premium.

There are times when many educators despair of the way in which the service is financed. Educational policies seem to be of secondary importance. No longer is it the universal practice to try to determine policies most likely to benefit the individual or the nation and subsequently to find the money to put them into effect. Occasionally individuals give the impression that they would prefer local government to spend no money at all on parts of the service and relatively little on other parts. Perhaps the problems of administering education would be fewer if the service were financed in a different way, possibly independently of other local government services. However, the history of education finance in this country, which cannot be described even briefly here, offers no simple solutions in spite of the variety of methods of financing used since local authorities assumed wide educational responsibilities in 1902. Moreover, without the financial strength of the educational service, local government as we know it might cease to exist.

10

Principles for Evaluation

Evaluation is the art and science of judgment and appraisal. Evaluation is a part of a larger cycle which begins with the formulation of objectives followed by the development of programmes to achieve the objectives wherein the process of teaching and learning is at work. The cycle is completed with the judgment and appraisal of the results. This cycle is a continuum, for the results of the process of appraisal trigger the examination and reformulation of objectives.

In recent years a new point of view has emerged regarding the testing and measuring process in the system of the schools. The emphasis on exact measurement of achievement has decreased as the result of increased understanding of the multiple facets of evaluation. The concept of exact measurement of various identifiable elements as the sole method of evaluation has given way to a concept of measurement as only one of many of the techniques of appraisal. And whereas evaluation was formerly seen as a final act of judgment it is now often regarded as a continuous process. The rather narrow use of evaluation, as specific measurement of student progress, has broadened to include appraisal of the strengths and weaknesses of the educational system itself so that, when properly applied, the process of evaluation is itself an influencing factor in achieving progress for the pupil, for the teacher, and for the administrator. Measurement then, is but one technique of evaluation. Other techniques and tools will include personal inventories (self-appraisal), rating (appraisal by others), conferences, interviews, tests, and projective techniques.

Evaluation in terms of appraisal and judgment is concerned with two elements of the school: the product of the enterprise—achievement of the student in learning; and the process of the enterprise—the school system's achievement of the objectives of the programme.

PURPOSES OF EVALUATION

Evaluation is a tool to be used to further the achievement of students in the attainment of the goals of education. It is one of the techniques which may be applied in the guidance and development of boys and girls. It is not alone a technique for appraising status and passing judgment on the achievement of boys and girls; it may also be a medium through which the student may be helped to attain his goals. In addition, it is a medium through which the school may identify its success or failure in achieving its purposes and goals. Evaluation includes classification and measurement, but it does not stop there. Among its many uses in the educational process, evaluation may accomplish:

1. Identification of the needs of students.
2. Stimulation of process of student self-appraisal and self-analysis.
3. Identification of class achievement at the end of a unit of work.
4. Motivation of the student to greater achievement.
5. Reappraisal of teaching methods.
6. Identification of the usefulness of programme materials.
7. Identification of the effectiveness of curriculum organization.
8. Appraisal of adequacy of facilities and equipment.
9. Identification of the degree of student achievement toward institutional objectives.

10. Unification of teaching and testing to lead the student toward greater self-analysis and self-responsibility.

Current practice does not always reflect effective use of evaluative techniques. The main use of evaluation often seems to be the testing and measurement of the student. The "hurdle" system of education, with its progressive steps in terms of subject matter conquered and grades passed makes student achievement of maximum concern. Students are grade-conscious, and with good reason. Evlauation is most commonly thought of as the examination period. Teachers think of the preparation and correction of test papers; students think of cramming the study and the ordeal of the test. Both tend to feel that the student alone is the object of evaluation, that the student is the one to be tested.

But by the concept of evaluation proposed here the process is something more than the measurement and testing of a student's degree of absorption of subject matter content. In the broader context, the process whereby the educational objectives are implemented is also being tested, and the purpose of such testing is the specific improvement of instruction. Improvement is desirable in order that student achievement may be greater, in order that the product of the process may more nearly represent the result which was intended.

PRINCIPLES FOR EVALUATIVE PROCEDURES

Certain principles may be used as a standard for evaluative procedures, much in the way a yardstick is used to determine line measurement. A programme of evaluation that is effective and efficient will apply each of the following principles.

The Appropriate Tool for that which is to be Measured should be Consistently Applied

Adherence to this principle insures a reliable result. For example, if a person wants to know the weight of a sack of potatoes, he does not use a yardstick to determine the number of pounds. He uses a scale to measure weight and a yardstick to determine a linear measurement.

Whenever Possible, Identifiable Elements must be Isolated and the Component Parts Measured

For example, if a teacher seeks to measure a student's skill in horseback riding he will separably judge the student's ability to set a walk, to post a trot, to sit a canter.

The Fact that the Whole is Greater than the Sum of its Parts must be taken into Account in the Final Summation of Measurement

To continue with the illustration used above, the skill of riding is greater than the simple addition of the abilities to ride at a walk, trot, or canter. The true test is the rider's reaction and skill in an unknown or emergency situation. Here is the added plus that defies isolation and identification. Here is an intangible, an element that is in essence "greater than the sum of its parts." This plus factor must be considered in any evaluative procedure.

Evaluation should not be Concluded Until All Applicable Measurement has been Considered

When judgment is made with important elements lacking, the picture is incomplete and the evaluation procedure is less accurate than it should be. For example, when a grade in physical education is based on attendance and effort, much of the available data has *not* been collected. Skill tests, knowledge tests, game ability tests, interpretive judgment tests, and the like are sources for more comprehensive evaluative data.

In Measurement, Data must be Interpreted in the Light of the Objectives which are Sought

Data which is unrelated to the purposes which are to be achieved is irrelevant and useless. If the purposes of course of study are listed as the development of skill in individual sports and the grade for the course is based on attendance and a battery of strength tests, the relationship of the data collected to the purposes of the course is obscure, to say the least. The evaluative process must relate measurement of the achievement in terms of the objectives which are sought.

The Goals of the Educational Continuum must be Kept Constantly in Perspective

There are various phases in the evaluation cycle. Evaluation is a continuous on-going process marked by periodic episodes. Each phase of the cycle has relationship with the other phases, and this continuum should be recognized. The cycle runs in this manner:

Goals are set (objectives).
Plans are devised to achieve the goal (Programme).
Guidance, Instruction, practice, take place (teaching).
Tests are applied to determine achievement (evaluation).
In the light of test results, new goals are set or old goals revised.
Plans are devised to achieve the goal.
Guidance, instruction . . .

This process of educational continuum must be constantly applied. The process of evaluation is never finished. It permeates all parts of the cycle.

EVALUATION AND OBJECTIVES

During the first quarter of the twentieth century anthropometric tests and measurements constituted a considerable portion of the physical education programme. There was rather general interest in the isolation and identification of measurable elements, and the ease with which these elements were measured tended to cloud the issue of their relationship to general objectives. As Williams noted: "In the face of devoted efforts to secure measurable outcomes, such as speed in running or height in jumping, there is the tendency to neglect the social justification for running or jumping . . . . The obviousness of the measured outcome often hides the indirect values in a situation."

The second quarter of the century saw physical education teachers, together with their educator colleagues, recognizing the insufficiency of a mechanistic concept of measurement. The logic of relating evaluation to the professional objectives was accepted. The lag in practice has been due in some measure to the considerable complexity of human behaviour and its motivation and in some measure to the use of tools inadequate for accomplishing qualitative evaluation.

There has been considerable effort on the part of educators to promote the idea of relating evaluative procedure to all of the professional objectives. They have urged that batteries of skill and knowledge tests be augmented with qualitative judgments and appraisal and that the process of evaluation become a more integral part of the teaching method. Oberteuffer has supported this approach. He says that there must be ". . . an alteration of traditional patterns in physical education. Neither skill, performance, nor exercise will be considered sufficient as outcomes of the physical education experience. Knowledge, behaviours and understanding will have to be added." He goes on to say that the class period cannot be devoted entirely to the teaching of skills. It will be important to take some time out for discussion. Problems arising in the class situation need to be reviewed and noted at the teachable moment. The physical education class needs to move closer to the laboratory experiences of other sciences, where the activity is performed for the purpose of examining and analyzing what happens during the performance. Such an approach will mean loss of some of the distinctive "exercise" atmosphere. It will mean some gain in greater realization of the integrated contribution the play experience has to make the human growth and development.

EVALUATION AND MEASUREMENT

It should be clear that measurement of isolated units of the whole does not comprise a true evaluative picture. A composite, the plotting of these isolated segments on some graph which can unify and present a related whole, is necessary for a fair comprehension of the subject.

There are two main kinds of measurement which need to be combined when evaluative judgments are made. Measurements of the quantity, degree, and amount of an element are called quantitative; those which judge the quality of an element are designed qualitative.

Quantitative Measurement

Certain components of a skill or knowledge which can be isolated lend themselves to quantitative measurement. This type of measurement is more common because it is easier. Educators have objective tools available for this type of measurement, and considerable experience in their use.

Isolation of variables is the very basis of scientific control. Where an element can be identified, such as learning facts about the rules of a game, its courtesies and etiquette, or its history, then the amount of that element can be measured. The student can list so many of the rules, is aware of certain do's and don'ts, knows such and such facts. With this data the teacher can give the student a grade; the student has learned a certain percentage of the total amount required. Or, in the matter of skills, so many balls can be thrown at a target of certain dimensions and the percentage of misses and hits can be scored; or the student can jump a certain height or a certain number of times, or run at such and such a speed for a particular distance. Such performance can be measured in quantity. However, when the quality of the performance becomes a factor of importance another facet has been added; while quantitative measurement may yield some data in this regard, certain other techniques must also be applied to produce an evaluation which includes the element of quality.

Qualitative Measurement

Qualitative evaluation requires the use of observational and judgment techniques. The judgment of growth and development where growth is incomplete requires a kind of measurement different from the measurement of a finished product. In qualitative evaluation the observer or examiner is concerned with attitudes, interests, special abilities, behaviour, hopes, aspirations, qualities of personality, value judgments, citizenship, and the like.

The more interdependent the factors which are to be measured, and the less capable they are of isolation, the more difficult is the process of evaluation. Exact quantitative determination required uniformity and repetition. But human beings are not machines capable of exact repetitive performance. Hence qualitative measurement is a more difficult appraisal, and much further study and research is needed before reliable instruments are available.

EVALUATION AND MOTIVATIONAL CLIMATE

Evaluation is a Key Factor in the Motivational Climate and Essential to the Guidance of Boys and Girls

Evaluation is not merely a matter of appraising status and passing judgment; it is a process through which the individual is helped to move from his present position or state to an improved one. This process is the development of self-appraisal and the induction of a motivational climate. Evaluation has been emphasized as a comprehensive term and, in this wider concept, the matter of self-appraisal is as important as teacher appraisal. In the modern school the two are closely interwoven. This section, therefore is concerned with the motivational climate and the relationships of this state with the practice of tests and measurements, with the process of evaluation of student progress.

Woodruff says:

> Since all development and learning are built from within the individual through his own self effort, and since it is psychological fact that each person's actions are determined by his own motivational machinery, it is difficult to avoid the conclusion that good motivational health is the single most important factor in development. It is almost the one factor with which learning and development cannot go on.

The student who is active, alert, and curious will find out for himself what makes the world go round. It is practically impossible to prevent a person with good motivational health from learning and developing. No examination is necessary as a whip to spur one on to learning in this circumstance. All teachers have known students who, in spite of dull teaching, dull books, inadequate background, and a hundred other obstacles would not accept half-knowledge for an answer or fall into a pattern of apathy and listlessness. They have known, too, the pupil with lack of motivational health, who cannot be dragged into a state of learning by any device now known, except that device which first arouses in him a state of active curiosity.

Motivational health may be cultivated. Motivational climate can be established. Beneficial experience in such cultivation, according to Woodruff, consists of three phases. In the first the individual must be aroused from within. This phase is ordinarily associated with a feeling of inadequacy which becomes to some degree intolerable. In the second phase, exploratory and consummatory activity is pursued leading to achievement. This phase of experience must follow the direction indicated by the arousal. The third phase is one of consolidation of gains and their orientation into the person's whole being.

It is important to note that in the first phase the arousal must be genuine and felt by the individual as a response to inadequacy. There can be no artifice; arousal cannot be effective if imposed from without. In the second phase, skilful teachers cannot be content to supply books and study materials. The process of exploratory and consummatory activity is one of guidance. Guidance means direction in the path of profitable progress toward the goal arousal has indicated. In the third phase, guidance involves reorientation of the student in an enlarged world, and here, because the learner has changed and his interests have changed, a new vantage point has been reached for new arousal of interests, and a new cycle of learning begins.

Since relative difficulty is experienced by most teachers in arousing students, or in recognizing the indications of aroused interest, a host of artificial incentives have been devised. Relying on such incentives, many schools hobble painfully along feeling dependent on a pattern of grades, examinations, promotions, honours, and punishments as the stimulus for learning. Teachers emphasize the incentives in grades, and then wonder why students work for grades, lamenting the lack of intellectual curiosity and lack of interest in knowledge for knowledge's sake. The schools are not alone in this.

Community organizations bolster attendance by a door prize, almost every philanthropic drive requiring gifts has the added advantage of a chance on some valuable prize. The values inherent in attendance or in giving, are assumed not to be sufficient in and of themselves for an effective appeal.

There is another facet to consider in the concept of rewards and incentives. The use of the word "award" usually carries the connotation of extrinsic, material or symbolic, artificial, some element not inherent within the activity for which it is presented. Rewards need not be essentially extrinsic or artificial. Psychologists use the term reward to mean the relief of a motivating tension. In these terms we can recognize that many activities do carry their own rewards. The satisfaction of a job well done, of a task completed, which is the release of the motivating tension—this in itself has significance and meaning. The reward is not always an extrinsic factor.

In line with the confusion which develops with the use of incentives one illustration will suffice. Woodruff suggests that there is an important difference between solving a problem for the sake of getting a deeper understanding of a principle and solving a problem for the sake of the teacher's approval. A gold star, for example, would be an artificial reward for the solving of the problem, but it would also symbolize the teacher's approval. The probable truth of the matter in this situation is that the student is learning how to win approval, not how to become a good problem-solver, and that teachers who use reward so as to encourage their students in a desire for approval or recognition have sidetracked the student in his basic motivational development.

It would seem to be a part of morality to teach not only the how and why of things but also the reason for doing things, the satisfaction which is inherent in the values of the activities themselves. If students are led to do things for values which are associated elsewhere they are being misled and taught falsely. Oberteuffer says: "When rewards in physical education are used to help the student face the realities of life, achieve something, organize and integrate values, then they are moral instruments. When they warp values, teach false values, distort ego, and dissipate energy, then they must be thought of as immoral."

If and when incentives are to be applied, Woodruff suggested that they meet the following conditions:

1. Their use should be restricted to such times are characterized by the student's having no initial interest in an activity in which he must engage.
2. The activity should be conducted in such a way that it contributes sufficient enjoyment and satisfaction on its own merits as to progressively make the artificial incentive less prominent and less important.
3. As soon as possible the artificial incentive should be dropped and the natural motivation of the activity used in its place.

When teachers really set out to implement the ideal of more effective education in terms of the findings of the physical and social sciences, the matter of artificial incentives will dissolve of its own weight. No man chooses the artificial when his alternative possibilities centre in the real thing. True motivational health will discard the necessity, real or imagined, of artificial incentives.

EVALUATION AND SELF-APPRAISAL

The Physical Education Programme Activities should Provide Essential Experience Opportunities for Accurate Self-appraisal

If education is to help the individual to come into increasing possession of himself and his powers, the motor activities of the physical education programme present an excellent laboratory in which experience in such self-appraisal may be accomplished. Successes or failures at play are there for everyone to see, and the measurement of success is rather generally objectively accurate. There is little anyone can do about a final game score, a completed dive, a fumbled ball, an arrow that has missed the target, a race that is won or lost. The individual knows where he stands; his peers and his observers also know. The lessons to be learned by those who cover up, explain, alibi, or graciously accept victory or defeat, by participant and for observer, are legion. The experiences associated with play can help students learn that they are neither better nor worse than they are. False concepts of superior worth or of worthlessness are equally poor. Accurate self-appraisal is a revitalizing tonic.

The challenge of responsible leadership is high here. Guidance in self-appraisal requires great skill, understanding, and integrity on the part of the teacher. It also requires gentleness and sensitivity. Students must be helped to face reality, and to do this requires perspective. This is the essence of mature leadership, to temper the bleakness of bald facts with the equity of considered relativity. Excellence can be enriched with modesty and failure to achieve with knowledge that one still belongs to the human race. Defeat need not mean disgrace.

The limited scope of the physical education programme has all too often contributed to false appraisal for students who could not achieve moderate success. Such students have been judged inept and incapable on the sole basis of the two or three sports taught throughout an entire school year. The programme must be broad enough to allow ample opportunity for the majority to find success in the variety of activities which rightly belong in the curriculum.

One reason why millions of American in adult life play the role of spectator rather than of participant in sports may be that the physical education which was theirs was too meager. It was less than meager, for many were on starvation rations. Calisthenics, perhaps team sports for the varsity athletes, desultory classes in a mish-mash of activities offered only when the gymnasium was available: this was the "programme". Self-appraisal under these conditions is, at best, unrealistic. And so, the general conclusion for a large majority turned out to be, "Physical education is not for me. I'm not athletic. I don't belong." The leaders in physical education must provide programmes that will "fit" all kinds and conditions of men; programmes that will lift and challenge the spirit of the participants; programmes that will provide opportunities for self-appraisal that is realistic.

EVALUATION AND THE GRADING PROCESS

Factors Implicit in Grading

Grading or marking is the more formalized part of the evaluation process, wherein a student is ranked in his individual achievement by the use of a symbol, numerical or alphabetical. Individual progress is generally measured in terms of one or a combination of many of the following criteria.

1. Improvement. A student may be ranked or graded in terms of his improvement or lack of improvement by measuring his beginning performance and, later, his performance following a period of instruction. At the beginning of the course or unit he is tested in certain measurable elements to determine his starting point. At the end of the course or unit he is retested in terms of his present performance in these same elements. The degree of difference marks his improvement in the aspects measured, and he is graded in terms of this measured progress or regression.

2. Peer Group Comparison. A student may be graded in terms of a comparison of his performance with that of other members of his class, his peer group. This is probably the most common standard for the assignment of grades. Here the same test is applied to each class member's performance and the results are combined in a rank order list. Then, in terms of a student's position on the scale, a letter or number symbol is assigned to his performance. Thus he is graded in comparison with his peer group.

3. Objective Standard. A student may be graded in terms of an objective standard, an achievement that has been established in one or two ways: by the establishment of norms on a national scale, or by the absolute achievement, the perfect score obtainable.

When national norms are used as a standard, the performance of the student is compared not only with his peers in his own class or school but also with the achievement of thousands of others in situations as nearly comparable to his as possible. This widens the base of comparison and in so doing makes for more objective evaluation of those elements which have been measured.

When the objective standard of absolute achievement or perfect score is used, the student is rated against the best that can possibly be achieved. In some circumstances the discrepancies between student score and perfect would be so great as to be ridiculous and have no meaning whatsoever; in other circumstances a comparison against the 100 per cent mark would be quite in order and be useful in accurate appraisal of performance.

4. Potential Performance. A comparison may be made in terms of the individual's performance against his capacity to achieve. This is one of the more difficult ways of grading because of the lack of adequate techniques or instruments for measurement of capacity. Subjective judgment comes into the picture and it is used with varying degrees of validity and reliability by examiners with varying degrees of competence in this regard. Quite commonly teachers ascribe a grade under this heading as a judgment in terms of effort, assuming that if a person really tries, his performance will reflect the limits of his capacity. The corollary to this is the belief that the student who really work to the limits of his capacity should not be penalized by a low grade should his performance prove inferior in comparison with peer group of objective standards. The use of this standard is controversial. Many feel that the approach is unrealistic; that results, not effort, are the only elements that may justifiably be measured.

Principles in Grading

A Combination of Many Grading Factors should be Used for Higher Validity and More Effective Evaluation

The grading process should make provision for evaluating each of these factors: improvement, peer group comparison, objective standard, and potential performance.

Testing should be Positive Education Rather than Negative Education

The testing programme is not designed as a battleground for the resolution of conflict between teacher and student. The purpose of testing is positive education in terms of an opportunity for evaluation of progress, detection of faults or misconceptions, and the correction of such faults. To "test 'em and leave 'em" is to miss the true purpose of testing. Tests should be spaced to allow time for reteaching and for correction. The common practice of giving final examinations on the last day of the class meeting fails to take account of this purpose of testing and reflects a negative rather than a positive approach in this regard.

Evaluation should Appraise both Product (Student Achievement) and Process (Institutional Achievement)

Evaluation appraises the excellence or fault of teacher and pupil alike. The teacher and his methods, the student and his achievement, the school and its organization are each inevitably concerned with the achievements of the other. The interrelationships cannot be ignored in judging the results of a testing programme.

Good Motivational Climate should make Grading a Part of the Teaching Process

Methods are interrelated-with evaluative procedures in terms of motivational health and self-appraisal. Good motivational health makes testing a part of teaching and self-testing and self-appraisal an antidote for cramming, grade consciousness, and examination-whip techniques.

EVALUATION AND THE EDUCATIONAL PROCESS

Appraisal is always a matter of comparison. It is important that comparisons be made with the right standards. In terms of the educational process, if a school board examines a number of neighbouring schools to determine the scope and programme of the physical education department and finds that all the programmes examined are similar to the programme in their own school, are they justified in assuming that their programme is a good one? If a person finds that several other people agree with his ideas, does that make the ideas valid? It is good research technique to test the "goodness' of a complex substance by looking at several samples? Is not anything more accurately appraised by examining its various components to see whether or not they are in truth what they are claimed to be and that they together combine to make an honest whole? So it is with programme evaluation. What are the objectives of the programme? On examination are the various components related to the organic whole? Is the programme in truth achieving what it claims to achieve?

Evaluation for the purpose of gaining information about the process of education will examine the criteria which have been established for each component of the process and see in what degree the achievement "measures up." One of the components of the process is the teacher. The characteristics of a true teacher constitute a yardstick by which to measure the teacher's qualification and performance. Another component of the process is the administrator. The attributes of a good administrator constitute criteria for measurement and evaluation, The duties of an administrator and also the principles for administration in terms of relationships with personnel and in terms of programme organization and operation constitute measurable items, either quantitative or qualitative. Each is important in the complete evaluation of the educative process. The process of education includes all of the aspects of programme organization and operation, all of the procedures by which individual or group outcomes are achieved.

The evaluative process must be continuous. Since it is a complex process, procedures should be established whereby a cycle of examination is developed. Each aspect of the process should then come under review in a constant and continuous cycle of examination, evaluation, revision, and correction. New method, new concepts of the needs and interests of individuals, new research data, new challenges for community and national life provide a constant prod to the educational process and highlight the need for review and revision. No educational programme can be meaningful or effective, can meet the needs of its participants, without continuous evaluative procedures.

11

Statistics, Record-keeping and Administration

THE ADMINISTRATIVE NEED FOR NUMERACY

The collection and maintenance of records and the preparation of statistical information is essential to administrative planning and the monitoring of performance. To say, however, that an educational administrator must be capable of a numerate approach to his work is not in any way to deny or belittle the qualitative human and educational aspects of his task. There is perhaps nothing more provoking than to be asked when putting forward a proposal, 'Is this suggestion being made on purely administrative grounds or is it made on educational grounds?' That question calls for—and has received—the response that it assumes a quite false dichotomy. Every educationally sound proposal will have resource implications which have to be assessed numerately by the interpretation of available data, as well as by the less objective factors, human and political, that must be taken into account along with legal constraints. Nor must one be lured into the presumption that because a problem can be wholly or partially defined in numerical terms it is capable of a unique or 'right' solution. In practice, a choice of solution must be made—based on the data, information and other factors which are known or can be assembled and interpreted within the time available for the decision-making process, of which an increasing proportion will nowadays be occupied in consultation.

The selection of relevant data and information is as important as its compilation. The school boy's Euclidean model problem—'given: to prove: proved' may be a useful training in intellectual rigour, but in no way mirrors life's real problems which call for a balancing of the advantages and disadvantages of alternative solutions which are logistically and politically possible. To sort out the relevant data and recognize the gaps in the data available are equally important. Gaps are inevitable not only because of manpower limitations and past omissions in the recording processes but because future developments, yet unknown, will produce fresh data which will amend the best possible forecasts and projections which can yet be made. In such cases the administrator looks for branching options—options capable of evolutionary change as further data becomes available.

DATA AND INFORMATION

It is natural to slip quickly into the use of these terms 'data' and 'information' and to adopt the respectable distinction between them, i.e. that 'information' is processed 'data'. Records are, loosely, the stuff that data is produced from and 'statistics' can consist of anything from agglomeration of more or less unprocessed data to a collection of useful and carefully presented information. This distinction between data and information is important: it is not new, though it has more recently been given added strength by the new breed of management experts. It was always there in the days before data processing and computers began to affect our lives so profoundly. The job of political adviser or statesman to a Tudor court was to collect his data and process it before presenting it to his master as 'information'. Of course his master had a shrewd idea of the data selection that had taken place, and his personal knowledge of his adviser's qualities would colour his view of the validity of the processing that had occurred. The adviser, it is true, was disciplined in the knowledge that too overt a departure from rigour or objectivity could have fatal results. If those processes are taken over by expensive electronic machines and the information presented in computer print-outs or visual display, it is unwise to credit it with a spurious validity. With all these electronic processes, there are similar opportunities for error in selection and interpretation.

WHAT RECORDS SHOULD BE KEPT?

A major question which the Chief Education Officer must answer at an early stage is what records should be kept, what data should his office extract from the records which are available or can be established, and what management information does he wish to formulate from it. There is always a danger that this question will be answered only by the momentum of the administrative process without proper regard to need. It is quite possible to allow records, data and statistical compilation of facts to proliferate, and the first and obvious essential is to ensure that the work undertaken is related to some specific need and is kept in proportion to the priority to be attached to that need.

An attempt is made in the following section to distinguish groups of data and information in relation to the purpose for which they are collected; the overall extent of the data and information with which an Education Department is normally involved is discussed in the last section of this chapter. This data and information may be financial or non-financial. A high proportion of it will be required for management purposes either locally or nationally and many of the records and data will be used for both financial and non-financial information. For example, returns of teaching staff and pupil numbers are used to calculate overall pupil/teacher ratios and the size of teaching groups—non-financial which relates to the standard of educational provision. This same data, however, coupled with budgetary control processes, will produce information on the average salaries of specific groups of teachers and unit pupil costs. The combination of this non-financial and financial information will influence staffing policies and assist management in the determination of policy options for future years.

Some records and data should be kept processed regularly to meet information needs which are not yet clearly recognized. Balanced judgement is required to avoid wasteful and irritating exercises while at the same time ensuring that future management decisions or decisions as between policy options will not be prejudiced by lack of relevant information. Thus, for example, in 1987 when the LEA Training Grants Scheme was introduced it was necessary for many authorities to define for the first time measures of the output and effectiveness of the INSET provided in order to justify the specific grants. Several authorities resorted to buying in computer packages developed for this very purpose.

The Chief Education Officer will need to keep abreast of the changing requirements for different data in response to changing national concerns. In the 60s and 70s LEA were largely obsessed with the logistical problems of accommodation and teacher supply. In the early 80s their preoccupations were falling rolls and financial constraints. Curricular matters were substantially delegated under central government's own model 'Articles of Government', nominally to governing bodies but in practice to the heads of schools. The latter half of the decade has seen LEAs and others seeking greater influence over the curricula available to pupils, especially in the 14-18 age range. This has led to the need for detailed curricular data to enable not simply the monitoring of change but also the provision of staff directly linked to an authority determined curriculum. At the same time, the Training Commission (at that stage the Manpower Services Commission) has resourced and influenced the introduction of a wider range of courses in many schools under the TVEI. This initiative has brought its own requirements for data collection in relation to the curriculum in order that the LEA, as part of its contract, may secure the funds from the Commission. This continuing interest of others in the curricula of schools is evident in the terms of the 1988 Education Reform Act with the introduction of a National Curriculum, where the LEA's role will be to monitor its detailed provision. The need for developing data collection systems in relation to the curriculum will, as a result, continue to figure high in LEA priorities.

It is also necessary to form a judgement as to whether data needs to be extracted on a continuous year-to-year basis or may be extracted on a 'one-off' basis for a particular task. Judgement is required as to the balance between the administrative effort and expense involved and the likely use to be made of the data. It may be relatively simple to record data on a day-to-day basis and therefore worthwhile doing so, even though reference to it for information purposes is likely to be occasional or some uncertainty exists as to the use to be made of it. There is clearly a special need for review of any practice of this kind from time to time.

THE RANGE OF MATERIAL

It is not proposed to attempt to catalogue the wide variety of statistics and records produced in an LEA office. Since the education service is locally administered, they do of couse form the data base of virtually all the information published nationally, though a good deal of the data may be processed elsewhere (especially, for example, at the DES and Chartered Institute of Public Finance & Accountancy) before being presented as information. In addition to the last section of this chapter, indicating the range of data and information processes in an education office, provides a guide to the information which is available nationally.

It is possible to distinguish broad purposes for which records are maintained and information prepared. These categories are, however, not mutually exclusive, since the results of much of this work will be used for more than one purpose.

1. Many records must be maintained for purposes of day-to-day administration—much of this work being done within the educational institutions themselves, though in such cases a good deal of the information will be needed centrally, both for those parts of the day-to-day administration which are centrally managed, and for other management purposes. Staff, student and pupil records will be required for a whole range of needs related to the management of the institution itself. Staff

records and required centrally or at area level for salary assessment and payment, superannuation and absence records, etc. Indeed, the personnel management function within a single large LEA is a major undertaking, extending as it does to the needs of tens of thousands of teaching and non-teaching full-time and part-time staff.

Where fees are chargeable, e.g. for further education students or boarding pupils, they must be assessed and invoiced. Meals must be paid for and free meals recorded, much of this work being performed at institutional level, subject to LEA financial controls and audit. Records of live births, age groups of pupils in school and under school age, records and forecasts of completion of housing units and of population movements, and records of school accommodation under construction or planned, are required for year-by-year decisions about admissions to schools as well as for decisions relating to the LEA's capital programme of building, which may run to many millions of pounds per annum.

Data on 'extra-district' pupils or students (a student not properly to be regarded as the responsibility of the ratepayers of the LEA maintaining the institution in which the student learns is 'extra-district') is needed to control the process by which one LEA pays another for services provided on its behalf.

Records of commitments under headings of capital and revenue expenditure must be maintained for budgetary preparation and control.

2. Data is also required for the formulation of policy options. Much of it derives from a process of the records maintained for day-to-day administrative purposes and a great deal of the information which finds its way into the nationally published DES or CIPFA statistics is of this kind. Projections of pupils and student numbers are essential to teaching and non-teaching resource planning and to the formulation of practical options for the organization of the educational system. The absence of information can pose difficulties, as can its

proliferation. Attempts to develop sound methodology for determining further education teaching and non-teaching costs (especially staffing and equipment costs) per student full-time equivalent and premises costs per student place, represent an endeavour to fill such an information gap which is widely recognized.

3. Information to also required for performance review. Records within the establishments are necessary for the educational and career guidnace of pupils, students and parents. Overall records of the qualifications being sought by pupils, students and parents and of their achievements help to monitor the contribution which the educational system makes to the country's economic and social welfare. The need for information for the monitoring of performance arises not only for management purposes, but from political considerations. Expenditure by LEAs on the education service is of the order of £14,000 million annually and the LEAs, being accountable to the public for this expenditure have a duty to demonstrate, so far as is practicable, that their use of this resource is reasonably efficient and productive. It is not possible, as with manufacturing, or marketing, or commercial or service industry, to strike a profit and loss account and assess performance in this way. But the process of commanding such a share of the nation's resources demands that reasonable public confidence is maintained. This process does not and cannot depend wholly or mainly on statistical data, but such data has its part to play. Public examination results in relation to age group sizes, levels of basic skills attainments, unit costs, staffing ratios, and levels of administrative cost in relation to total expenditure, are examples of areas in which the measurement of performance is important in the political sense as well as in respect of the more direct administrative need. So far as public examination results at 16 and 18 are concerned, LEAs have a statutory duty to ensure that they are published in respect of their maintained schools and the 1988 Education Reform Act

establishes procedures for the publication of attainment tests at various ages.

4. A substantial volume of the statistics with which an LEA is concerned is produced as a requirement of central government, but this nevertheless does not, perhaps with minor exceptions, constitute a separate category from those indicated above. There is a great deal of common ground between the DES and LEAs as to their needs for information, and indeed standing arrangements exist for them to review in some detail the information-gathering process both as to the content and methods. Educational policy determination at national and LEA level goes hand-in-hand—there are also standing arrangements for the DES and LEA associations to review policy options or, in these days of 'expenditure-led' decisions, at least to assess and monitor the policy implications of such decisions—so the common ground in their information requirements is based on common need. As indicated at (2) above, the substantial body of information contained in the DES annual statistical publication derives from LEA returns but it would be largely true to say that these returns, though required of LEAs by statute, can be seen by them in practice as a by-product of the LEA's own needs.

WHERE SHOULD RESPONSIBILITY LIE?

How should the work of collecting and processing data be organized? It is possible to argue for the creation of a central statistical group within an Education Department or indeed within an LEA. It is likely that most authorities will have given consideration to this matter and in particular will have attempted to assess the degree of common or inter-departmental use of data. If this were substantial, there would be a case for establishing a common 'data-base' on which the management information needs of departments could draw. In practice, it is found that the great majority of the data is required to meet a specific information need of a branch, and is specific to that branch. While, therefore, overlapping needs and functions must be recognized (as in the case, for example, with housing statistics and health statistics relating to live births), it remains generally true that responsibility for most data collection continues within the branch of the department with the major concern in the relevant area. That at least has the merit that the motivation of the staff involved is sharpened by their own management needs, but it is important that the inter-branch and inter-departmental communication referred to later in this chapter are sound so that any data separately collected by an individual department can be incorporated in a common data base where this is appropriate. At least it appears true that even where some centralization of statistical work has been implemented, much of the work remains in practice with the branches themselves. It is however important that it should be quite clear to the department as a whole where the responsibility for each area of data collection and processing lies and this is especially true of those areas such as basic school population forecasts which are required for a variety of purposes, including budget preparation and determination of staffing policies.

THE ROLE OF THE COMPUTER

It is also important that the department has a clear policy on the computerisation of data processing which recognizes both its value and limitations. A computerised management information system will not tell management what information is required. Computers, however, now play a major role in an LEA's work. The increasing use of microcomputers throughout departments means that their power is now often distributed away from the mainframe computer of the authority. The LEA's computer manager should possess a general view of the whole of the data collection and processing which is going on within the departments and of their information needs. There is a need for regular discussion of the ways in which he or she can both in the short term assist departments in their task within existing resource limits, and, in the longer term, determine what additional resources of manpower and equipment are required to meet the authority's needs.

Management information needs should be identified at the right level of management. Top management will identify what is required for decisions about policy options. These requirements are made known to middle management, who are themselves fully aware of the day-to-day collecting and processing needs for administrative purposes. The major responsibility for continuous appraisal between departments and the central computing system is thus best discharged at middle management levels. It is top management's responsibility to see that this appraisal process is maintained. That appraisal will need to have regard to the 'time critical' nature of much management information and the desirability of building into it a degree of flexibility which will permit a computerised system to produce more information from the data than may seem immediately necessary. These considerations are not unique to a computerised system. Even in the case of a simple manual return and analysis, the data needs to be assembled and handled in a way which enables a variety of selections and combinations to be made from it.

It is fair to ask whether there are any general considerations which will help to identify the work for which the assistance of the computer service would be sought. If good middle management communication is maintained, the question will be answered progressively from year to year and that communication will also serve to establish the extent to which a 'data base' should be established, a 'data base' being a group of records capable for use by all departments of an authority, as opposed to those held by branches in conventional files for specific purposes. Amongst other considerations which will govern the computerisation of data processing are, firstly, the amount of manipulation of data involved—an ad hoc return relating to a class technical equipment requiring replacement may be handled manually, but the establishment of an inventory or machine equipment by age and type and its regular up-dating with data linked to supply, maintenance and disposal procedures, could be a candidate for computerisation. A second consideration of some importance is the number of variables involved and the network linkage potential. For example, further education students' records will relate to college statistics and college resource needs, to overall LEA statistics and possibly to invoicing for fees. They also cover a wide variety of full-time and part-time students working at different levels in different learning areas. Limitations of resources will in practice mean that the selection of matters for which computer assistance should be sought will depend generally on their priority and the likely cost effectiveness of the operation.

Examples of data processing for which computer services are currently used are:

1. School population records and forecasts including school leaver projections.
2. Local school accommodation and pupil numbers, records and projections.
3. Further education records and production of related statistics.
4. Further education awards, calculations of parental contributions, issue of grant letters and making of payments, and preparation of statistical management information.
5. Payroll work for—and increasingly the extraction of management information, including age and qualification structure of teaching force by subject areas.
6. School meals and catering—meal costs (food and overheads) and menu planning, for optimum cost and quality benefit.
7. Home to school transport route planning.
8. Careers guidance.
9. Secondary school selection procedures, where still in use—quantification of primary school records and assessments, calculating scores, and serial listing by schools and LEA.
10. School timetabling—at least to a first degree of approximation—the need for manual intervention is difficult, if not impossible, to avoid.
11. One-off applications, e.g. reading age or other attainment surveys, and analysis of returns required for special management needs.
12. Library work—cataloguing, ordering and circulation control.

13. Recoupment claims between local authorities.
14. Staff profiles—qualifications and experience—subjects taught and 'level' of teaching.
15. Energy usage and conservation measures for school buildings.
16. The transfer of information from LEAs to schools/colleges (e.g. budget allocations and latest expenditure profiles) and from schools/colleges to LEAs (manpower, pupil number, etc.) required to run schools/colleges operating under schemes of delegated management.

As the development of micro-electronics leads to the availability of comparatively cheap small computers, the degree of sophistication required of the system—especially the flexibility needed in the selection of combination of pieces of information required—is also a factor determining whether the application is best handled by access to a major central computer or by equipment available in the department or branch involved. Where continuous operation of set procedures is required, e.g. at collection and issue points at branch libraries or for staff and teaching space timetabling work within a school, including the storage and print-out or visual display of individual pupil's subject options and timetables, local equipment may be suitable although there is much to be gained from links to a major computer network.

It seems reasonable to assess the major changes following the development of micro-electronic techniques as arising from the fact that applications which could not be considered for a main computer centre for economic reasons can now be developed on micro equipment. This is still most profitable with processes requiring a comparatively low volume of data and it is necessary for other processes to link micro equipment to a major computing facility, with its capacity to store a massive data base to which the micro application needs access. As an example, the data volume required for secondary school accommodation and roll forecasts can be comparatively small. One element is the existing student capacity of the buildings. It is theoretically practicable to assess this from a major data base relating to all school premises and required for the purpose of care and maintenance, energy conservation and estate management. The development of such a data base, however, could set back initiation of the roll/accommodation forecast application for some years, and an interim exercise using existing departmental-based assessments of existing student capacity on micro equipment could well be feasible. As hitherto, the crucial question will be whether a computerised system, centrally based or otherwise, will justify its cost in terms of the value of the information produced. In any case the objective should be to provide facilities in education offices for access to management information from the central system and there should be facilities to withdraw files of information from that system and insert files into it from the separate smaller computers when necessary.

COMPUTERS—WHAT DOES THE ADMINISTRATOR NEED TO KNOW?

The senior manager's main need may well be one of attitude and background rather than technical knowledge. He needs to be aware of the potential of computer-assisted processes and to be sufficiently receptive to their adoption as to be able to assess or secure an assessment of their cost and efficacy, and to give the right degree of priority of investment costs. The techniques themselves will mainly be handled at middle management level and it is the middle level managers who, through their structured relationships with the computer management of the LEA, will initially identify most development possibilities. Nevertheless, top management must have sufficient knowledge to display a healthy curiosity which can trigger off fruitful lines of enquiry, as well as respond sympathetically and with knowledge to representation by middle management. For example, how much time do staff handling school accommodation problems spend in retrieval of information? At what point will it be fruitful and economic to provide slected staff with visual display units (requiring on-line facilities) to present such information and to train them to handle it? In other fields, e.g. major awards for students at universities and polytechnics, wherever the essential records are on a computer system, facilities for visual display of vital information (in this case, individual student's assessments) are always technically practicable.

In general, the need of senior managers is not for training in skills which, since they will not be practised, will quickly be forgotten. Nor is there a need for in-depth knowledge of computer technology, which is the province of the computer professional and which may be overtaken by continuing development. In-service training should be designed to generate awareness, and this implies obtaining sufficient knowledge of the fundamental principles of current computer development. For example, communication networks (e.g. the desirability or otherwise of linking colleges or area offices to a central system or to each other); data base facilities (the ability of several users to have access to a common pool of data) on-line information retrieval (how quickly is the information needed, and how up-to-date should it be?). The use of such a network could extend not only to the passing of stored information from one institution to another but to a more general interchange of messages through electronic mail in lieu of correspondence. This awareness can be achieved by periodic computer presentations at management seminars. Computer literature can be helpful, but it has drawbacks, such as its technical nature, the use of jargon and the inability to question or discuss its findings.

AN EXAMPLE—PRIMARY SCHOOLS ACCOMMODATION AND ROLLS

Earlier in this chapter it is pointed out that a simple heading in the list of area of work covered by data preparation and processing in an education office may deceptively mask a fairly complex area of work.

Heading 4 ('Premises—accommodation and rolls') of the final section of this chapter may be selected as such an example, this being an area in which there are clear advantages to be gained from computerisation of the system. The problem may be stated as the need to keep under review the accommodation and pupil rolls of some hundreds of primary schools within the LEA (secondary schools present a somewhat different problem requiring a different approach) with a view to assessing:

(*a*) the needs of schools for additional accommodation;
(*b*) the need for the provision of new schools;
(*c*) schools from which temporary accommodation may be transferred;
(*d*) staffing and accommodation needs which would be generated by alternative policies on class sizes and alternative staffing policies.

The input into this programme should include:

(*a*) details of the existing accommodation (this may in practice be derived from a central data base used for other departmental purposes);
(*b*) accommodation under construction or planned to start in an approved capital programme (with completion dates), including the effect of new schools to be opened in the area;
(*c*) an analysis of present school roll by age groups and class sizes;
(*d*) the year groups of children under school age already in the area and expected to seek entry to the school;
(*e*) planned future housing completions by size of dwelling unit—both local authority and private schemes;
(*f*) estimates of initial and subsequent 'school product' of these dwellings;
(*g*) historic and projected figures for net migration into or out of the school's catchment area; and
(*h*) the local practice in respect of the admission of children under statutory school age.

The computer programme can be designed to give a clear school-by-school print-out of the relevant management information and if carefully devised can give valuable information about the resource implications of different policy options. As so often with computerised systems, its introduction inevitably involves a new and carefully thought through discipline in the assembly and input of the information, ensures that problems common to large numbers of institutions are dealt with equitably and, subject to what is said below about interpretation, assures management that incipient difficulties which could be overlooked in a less regulated manual system are brought to light despite the scale of the exercises.

DECISION-MAKING

Management information systems, however sophisticated, are not a substitute for good management. It has already been pointed out that it is necessary to pose the right questions, to ensure that the data is available and to process the data soundly. A word now needs to be said about the interpretations of the resulting information and about decision-making. It is commonly said that you can prove anything by statistics. This is of course quite untrue, but you can deceive yourself inadvertently by the manner of presentation. You can also go seriously astray by false logic in the process itself or by failing to take into account the degree of accuracy of the original data. Faulty local secondary school roll projections, for example, led in the immediate post-war years to at least one school that was redundant almost before it was completed. In fact the short-term (six to seven years) projection of future secondary school rolls should, in theory, be relatively simple, since the children are already in the primary schools. No secondary school can, however, be matched with a precise set of primary schools and the effect of parental choice and of family movements, especially in newly developed housing estates, must be carefully and fully assessed. The impact on this of the Education Reform Act provisions for enhancing the ability of parents to fill schools to their physical capacity is still unclear but will certainly make planning by the LEA more hazardous.

It is also important to distinguish between long-term and short-term needs. It is a matter of historic fact, for example, and can also be demonstrated by a simple mathematical model, that a housing development carried out quickly—over a period of a few years—will show a short- to medium-term demand for primary school places, which is far in excess of the steady longer term need. The same development with the same family pattern of initial occupancy spread over a longer period will show a reduced discrepancy between medium-term and long-term needs. For example, a large estate developed in two years can, with a certain family pattern of initial occupancy, show a short-term need which is double the long-term need. The same estate and family structure spread over an eight-year construction period could produce a short- to medium-term need no more than about 25 per cent of the longer term numbers.

Statistics, data and information constitute essential management tools which like all tools should be used with skill and care. They will not do the job themselves. Good systems will both facilitate the general administration of an office, alert management to incipient problems and, within their own limitations, quantify them. The manager should know these limitations and in particular the degree of accuracy of the original data. In the primary school accommodation survey described above, for example, the data is known to be of variable accuracy and objectivity. The records of accommodation call for judgements as to the pupil capacity of buildings of different types. Projections of housing completions are notoriously subject to marked change because of planning and other technical difficulties, political and economic conditions and market fluctuations. Reliable figures for migration and children under school age are easy to come by. The responsible administrator will not commit himself to substantial capital expenditure on the strength of an uncritical look at a computer print-out. Before this step he will cross-check the strength of the data and the validity of the conclusion. With the lead time involved from the programme to the contract stage of building, he will need to update those conclusions from time to time, however irritating this may be to his architect colleagues. It may even be necessary, exceptionally, to write off abortive work and fees and pull out of a proposal at a late stage, if that is the sensible long-term decision.

In this example, as in many others, we live in a real world where the exercise of free will and the interplay of views of individuals and organizations dictate that decisions must be flexible and adaptable to changing circumstances. Firmness of purpose as to policy must not be confused with rigidity of thinking as to means. The late Frank Barraclough, a man not easily to be deflected from a policy aim once firmly grasped, and one who regarded the pre-determination of the 'abscissae and ordinates' of a problem as basic to its solution, would nevertheless place his hand on his heart and say to his young men, 'Whatever you think you've proved, and however much you may be convinced that the facts add up—if it feels wrong here—don't do it!'

RECORDS, DATA AND STATISTICS MAINTAINED REGULARLY OR AS REQUIRED BY LEA

Note: This list cannot be exhaustive and the categories inevitably overlap. The volume of information extracted from the data varies considerably. For example, the further education student records form the basis of virtually the whole volume of the DES annual statistics. The list is intended to serve as a guide to the range of the data prepared and maintained in an education office.

1. Teaching Staff

Establishments and numbers (full-time equivalent) in post, by total LEA, by area (if applicable), by schools or institutions, by type or grade of posts.
Age and training needs qualification structure.
Average salary levels, incremental 'drift'.
Probationary teachers, numbers and records.
Volume of attendance at in-service training and induction courses.
Leave of absence records for sick pay, etc.
Use of supply teachers.

2. Pupil and Student Numbers

Live births and total population figures for area and sub-areas (actual and projected).

Actual and projected school rolls, classified in age, for total LEA (for areas) and for individual schools.

Further education student population (classified by age, numbers and full-time equivalent) by mode of study, by courses pursued (levels and objectives) and by types of institution.

Pupils and students 'belonging to' other LEAs or to no LEA (for recoupment and pooling purposes).

Pupils with statements of special need: numbers and types of statement and types of placement (e.g. day and boarding, maintained, non-maintained and independent schools).

School attendance, non-attendance and exclusions.

3. Schools and Institutions and their Management

Number and types of schools, colleges and other institutions.

Size of registration and teaching groups.

Pupil/teacher ratios in schools and student/staff ratios in colleges.

Teacher staff establishments and numbers of teacher in post by school.

Proportion of AFF/NAFE total institutional costs in colleges.

College and course information—enrolment, objectives and attainments.

Examination attainments of school pupils.

Integrated courses, linked courses and industrial training courses.

Staff usage in colleges—actual and potential contact teaching hours and relief for non-teaching duties.

College/school interrelationship for 16-19 year olds; distribution and size of 'A' level courses.

Appointment, resignations and records of managing and governing bodies.

4. Premises

Accommodation and rolls—records and forecasts by LEA, by area and institution.

Building programmes—performance and monitoring.

Building maintenance, floor areas and cleaning costs.

5. Youth and Community and Careers

Numbers, types and usage of institutes, centres, camps and community centres.
Staffing establishments and posts filled.
Income and expenditure of institutions operating on net budgetary basis.
Participation records, youth and adult activities—centres—award schemes—adult literacy.
Employment statistics—vacancies—unemployment figures—average earnings.
Actual and projected numbers of school leavers.
Employment and further education destinations of school leavers.
Usage of Youth Training Scheme Programme.

6. Awards and Welfare

Financial data—numbers by type of award and unit cost to LEA.
Educational data—types of institution and course and student objectives.
Records required for pooling purposes and claims on DES for statutory awards.
Free meals records for schools and colleges.
Provision of clothing and school uniform.

7. General Administration

Manpower statistics.
Staffing establishments and numbers in post.
Payroll records and statistics.
Catering—school and college turnover and take-up.
Kitchen accommodation and usage.
Staffing and food unit costs for school meals.
Institutional catering costs—profit and loss.
Ground maintenance costs and data.

12

Personnel Management and Development

INTRODUCTION

Fourteen years have elapsed since the reorganization of local government. It is therefore appropriate to review changes which have occurred in that period, opening as it did with a mixture of anxiety and enthusiasm within the new Local Education Authorities, many much different from their predecessors, and all with different teams of education officers and advisers.

The structure for personnel management and development in the majority of new authorities was based upon their interpretation of the report of the Bains Committee. That report drew attention to the highly labour-intensive nature of local government and emphasized that the major way to improve its efficiency was through the more effective use of human resources. It considered that local government lagged behind industry in the recognition and development of personnel management.

In those early days of the new authorities there was a general tendency to establish a personnel department led by a chief officer or assistant chief officer, with direct access to the Chief Executive, whose specialist personnel knowledge would, it was believed, be accepted and acted upon by all departments. Education Departments, as the largest employers of staff within the local authorities, frequently felt threatened by the new centralist arrangements. In catering, grounds maintenance and cleaning they were often the largest operators in their area. They believed that then specialist officers had considerable experience and expertise in the management of large numbers of staff in specific service areas which supported the work of the schools and colleges for which they were also responsible. Furthermore, their personnel management experience had covered highly qualified professional staff in higher education, schools and colleges, together with educational psychologists, inspectors and advisers, education officers, careers officers and education welfare officers, plus many other kinds of staff such as technicians, nursery nurses and drivers. They were experienced too in the management of large numbers of part-time employees. Managers in the education service therefore had confidence in their ability to manage large numbers of staff in diverse areas of activity with a wide range of negotiating bodies and a variety of conditions of service.

It was hardly surprising therefore that there was a degree of resentment within education departments at what they saw as a usurping of their responsibility by a central department and a risk, as they saw it, that the total operation of the service might be threatened by insensitive and inexperienced handling of individual groups of staff in a highly complex service. Of particular concern was the transfer of responsibility for teachers, in a small number of authorities, from the Education Department and the Education Committee to the Personnel Department and the Manpower Committee or its equivalent. Education officers were reinforced in their view at the time by the 1977 SEO statement on the role of the Education Officer: 'Chief Education Officers are high calibre managers of very large human enterprises who have, as a central function, giving leadership to the authority's education service, including the staffs of its establishments; they give advice and support to all staff, teaching and non-teaching, in the performance of their duties . . . and contribute to their professional development or vocational training and generally promote their effectiveness'.

The reality of the situation however was somewhat different. A number of statutory enactments, introduced at or before local government reorganization, had had significant influence upon the personnel management by Education Departments of their large staffs. In applying that legislation they were increasingly dependent upon the expertise and guidance provided by central personnel departments who, quite properly, were concerned to ensure that the Council, as an employer, treated all employees equitably. This legislation included, for example, the Redundancy Payments Act (1965), Contracts of Employment Act (1972), Trade Unions and Labour Relations Act (1974), Health and Safety at Work Act (1974) and Rehabilitation of Offenders Act (1974), followed in close order after 1974 by the Employment Protection Act (1975), Sex Discrimination Act (1975), Race Relations Act (1976), Employment Protection (Consolidation) Act (1978), Employment Act (1980) and Employment Act (1982). Allied to this legislation was the emergence of a growing number of codes of practice at national level for local application, particularly in relation to equal opportunities and race relations and health and safety at work. There also emerged locally determined codes of practice in relation for example to equal opportunities, redeployment and early retirement for teachers. At the same time there was an increasing demand on the part of teacher associations for more precisely defined conditions of service based upon the Burgundy and Silver Books and for local negotiation of conditions of service in both schools and further education colleges.

Consistent with the legislation, there emerged complex procedures leading to industrial tribunals for employees having a grievance in relation to the termination of their employment or their failure to secure a post. Education officers and advisers found themselves increasingly involved in a world which was unfamiliar to them and within which they had to learn new skills, assisted by specialist colleagues in central departments, notably personnel and clerks.

A further significant factor has been the emergence of better trained and more active trade union representatives for both teachers and non-teachers. Education Officers cannot negotiate with non-teaching staff in their department in isolation since, particularly in the case of manual workers and APT and C staff, the issues involved may impact upon the conditions of service of similar staff employed by a number of other Council departments. In short, Education Officers have had to learn, if they did not know it already, that they do not operate in a vacuum but need to have regard to the overall staffing policies of the Council as employer. Furthermore, the production of quarterly figures for the manpower watch, identifying categories of employee and comparisons of the number employed year on year, has presented a form of accountability for the education service which has not always been comfortable for Chief Education Officers and their committees. The formula for calculating the full-time equivalence of part-time employees has worked to the disadvantage of Education Departments and the seasonal appointment of staff, particularly part-timers in the adult education service, has tended to inflate the figures and give rise to headlines about 'massive' staff increases which are far from reality: Education Officers have had to come to terms with increased public scrutiny of staffing levels in the education service.

THE MID-80s

The establishment in most authorities in the early years following local government reorganization of formal bodies for consultation and negotiation by Teacher Associations where they did not already exist has given Education Officers new experiences in the delicate process of local consultation and negotiation.

Practice has varied from authority to authority particularly so far as the involvement of elected members is concerned but the fact that these bodies exist presents a forum for teacher association representatives and officers to share a jointly formulated agenda on matters of interest to both parties. At the same time, many senior managers in Education Departments are part of a generic interdepartmental team of managers meeting with representatives of manual and APT and C staff in similar bodies established by the Council for its employees in all services. The separate approach required for teaching staff on the one hand and manual and clerical staff on the other has not always been easy for Education Officers, nor indeed for Personnel Officers, to come to terms with. The salary and conditions of service position of professional staff in the education service, for whom, generally speaking, the Education Departments have been responsible, compared with those for clerical and manual workers, for whom generally speaking, central departments have been responsible, has given Education Departments a degree of independence in relation to teachers that they have not enjoyed in relation to other categories of staff. This has sometimes given rise to interdepartmental difficulties arising from different treatment in terms of conditions of service between the two categories of employee.

Falling rolls have presented a whole new set of challenges for Education Department managers. Most authorities were obliged in the late 70s to negotiate with their Teacher Associations schemes for the management and deployment of the teaching force, initially in the primary schools and latterly in the secondary schools as a substantial reduction in the birth rate worked its way through the system. Redeployment of teachers has become an art from art form highly developed by education practitioners. Other devices for the effective management of a reducing teacher force have included retraining, particularly through one year secondments, and premature retirement with or without compensation. It is significant that a good number of authorities do not have similar procedures for non-teaching staff although those staff are increasingly vulnerable as the secondary school population reaches its trough.

The Houghton and Clegg awards for teachers and the link between Soulbury salaries and head teacher salaries had a profound effect upon the relativities within the service between professional Education Officers on the one hand, and advisers and head teachers on the other. Local Education Authorities have, in the past, frequently been unsympathetic to arguments advanced by Chief Education Officers that the relativities which were established in 1974 need to be maintained to secure the recruitment of young, high quality, experienced teachers into Education Departments. Compression of the span of salaries did not always assist Education Officers in the complex negotiations and consultations which they were undertaking with Teacher Associations, nor in their work with advisory and head teacher colleagues.

The weak relationship within the former Burnham Committee between salaries and conditions of service had remained an area of complexity and vagueness for many years. The culmination of this unsatisfactory state of affairs was the damaging teachers' dispute of 1986 and 1987 leading to the Secretary of State's decision to intervene. This has raised major issues for Teacher Associations and officers of LEAs in terms of the validity and future scope of local negotiation of conditions of service. One feature of the dispute was teachers' readiness to take unprecedented industrial action in support of their claim. It was perhaps a new experience for Education Officers to find themselves in a position in which there was virtually nothing that they could do by way of effective negotiation to alleviate the impact of teachers' industrial action upon the schools, whilst, at the same time, facing demands from the public and elected members to do something to end the disruption of children's education. The implementation by the Secretary of State of new conditions of service for teachers, together with some long overdue court judgements about the professional duties of teachers has eliminated a great many doubts, and LEAs are now clear about the major components of a teacher's professional duties and what action they can take in respect of individuals or groups of teachers who choose to refuse to carry out those duties.

Education Officers have had to prepare strategies for the management of the education service and personnel within it in a period of constrained resources but high expectations by staff and clients. The greater part of an Education Committee's budget is devoted to staff, both teaching and non-teaching. The demographic effects on the education service have created a need to reduce teacher and non-teacher numbers. Much staff reduction has been achieved on a year-on-year basis rather than in a planned and progressive way.

The pressure on manpower in Local Authorities has had its effects on central departments too. Increasingly, the tendency has been to shrink the size of central personnel departments to provide an advisory service rather than a full personnel service. Responsibility for personnel management has been passed back to some Education Departments often without the accompanying additional support staff to do the job. This of course is at a time when there is unprecedented activity in personnel matters relating to teachers and non-teachers.

THE FUTURE

The 1987 pay award for teachers, with its restructuring proposals, has created for Education Officers and head teachers a complex three- or four-year programme of structural development within schools. This requires skilled supervision and management following careful consultation or negotiation at authority and school level if the Secretary of State's targets are to be met and financial limits are not to be exceeded. The 1987 Manual Workers' pay award carried with it substantial implications for Education Department personnel managers, the effects of which will take some time to appreciate and implement but will certainly increase the costs to LEAs.

The requirement of the Local Government Act, 1988 that a number of local authority maintained services should be put out to competitive tendering during the course of 1989 to 1991 presents particularly significant challenges for education managers who cannot, in this regard, operate in isolation from other departments. The volume of personnel management will decrease, in some sectors significantly, if contracts are won by the private sector. LEAs now have to consider how the personnel function is to be undertaken where contracts are won by Direct Labour Organizations. What is clear is that the Direct Labour Organizations' staff will form part of the Education Department or Country Council's staffing depending upon arrangements determined within the local authority. No doubt different models will emerge but it is clear that the DLO could either provide its own personnel management structure or purchase from the Education Department the personal service it requires. It is perhaps too early to see what the implications might be of individual schools contracting out their own services under arrangements for the Local Management of Schools following the Education Act, 1988.

Councils, or their Education Departments, depending upon local arrangements, will have to address the need to provide staffing structures for the contractor side where their DLO is successful in securing contracts and, whether all or some of their services are contracted out to the private sector, they will have to develop an organization to fulfil the client roles of service specification, contract preparation and supervision of the contract. This raises important issues for the organization of an Education Department and the role which its personnel section plays in the process.

Some of the clauses in the Education Act, for example in relation to local management of schools and employment of staff, plus the establishment of grant maintained status, may well serve to shift the emphasis within Education Department personnel sections from the management of staff and indeed possibly the negotiation of conditions of service to an advisory and guidance role equivalent in relation to head teachers and governors to that played by central personnel departments in relation to Education Departments.

The Act moves much of the responsibility for the appointment, management and disciplining or dismissal of teachers firmly to school level. Those authorities which do not devolve responsibility for local management to schools with less than 200 on roll will continue to fulfil the functions which are currently their responsibility for those schools. At the same time, however, head teachers, principals and governing bodies will be looking to the LEA for advice, guidance and support in exercising their responsibilities under the Local Management of Schools Scheme. Education Departments' personnel and finance sections will have an important responsibility to produce guidelines and detailed documents of advice on employment and conditions of service legislation and good practice to assist heads, principals and governors to fulfil their functions at local level. There could be significant implications for the size and structure of Education Department personnel sections in the future as a result of this decentralization. Local authority staff, notably Education Officers and advisers who have day-to-day contact with schools and colleges and clerks to governors, where they are local government employees, will need greater expertise in these important matters if they are to give advice promptly and correctly when it is required at school and college level. There will need to be a re-evaluation of training requirements for senior staff in schools and Education Departments, and of the role of Education Department personnel staff.

Local authorities have been called upon by the Secretary of State to indicate in their schemes of local management of schools, the training programmes which they propose for teaching and non-teaching staff, governors and their own staff, to ensure that the scheme is implemented efficiently. For this, detailed consultation with Teacher Associations, governors and others involved is required to ensure that the programmes are relevant and purposeful.

STAFF DEVELOPMENT

1. Teachers

LEAs' responsibility for the training of their staff has always been an important aspect of their personnel management role. It is fair to say that in the case of most authorities far greater emphasis has been placed on training and retraining of teachers than it has on training and retraining of other categories of staff. The budget for professional staff training usually far exceeds that for non-teachers. The changes in the grant-related in-service training programme have influenced the structure, delivery and priorities of LEA's arrangements for in-service education and training, and will have the effect of equalising expenditure between authorities. This will benefit authorities who have not been able, in the past, to give as much attention to this important area of their work as others. The virtual elimination, following removal of access to the 'pool' for the purpose, of one year full-time secondments of teachers has not helped to assist the management of the reduction of the teacher force and other solutions are having to be found by education managers. As rolls began to rise again in the primary schools in many parts of the country, the pressures of contraction gave way to problems of recruitment including the need to retrain secondary teachers for primary work. Similar retraining needs may well emerge in the secondary schools in the late 90s in various parts of the country. Carefully planned staff development programmes including retraining to overcome curriculum mismatch amongst secondary teachers as rolls fall and to implement the National Curriculum, will certainly be required.

Training programmes for shortage subject areas have been evolved nationally and locally in an attempt to combat an increasingly serious problem. Competition from industry for scarce skills has continued to present problems for LEAs and their managers.

The introduction of an entitlement national curriculum for all pupils in all schools has added to the need for Government and LEAs to focus on long-term recruitment into and training within the teaching profession. The demand for an increased share of graduate physicists, chemists, mathematicians and modern linguists has been addressed by Government through the TASC [Teaching as a (Second) Career] Group. Incentive payments to certain shortage subject area graduates who enter a PGCE course has provided an initial attraction, although insufficient of those entering the course have actually gone on into teaching. General problems of recruitment into teaching, in part related to salaries, but also in part to the status and public image of the profession, along with particular problems in specific shortage areas, are being added to by two other factors. Firstly, there is a generally accepted view that pupil/teacher ratios in school will need to be improved to take account of the time teachers must spend on systematic periodic assessment of pupils throughout their primary and secondary careers, the maintenance of records of achievement for pupils, and the appraisal of teachers themselves. The other factor is that this need for improved recruitment into the teaching profession comes at the very time when there is a trough in the numbers of young people in the school leaving age groups. All employees, therefore, will be recruiting from a declining market, and the pressure on the graduate market is going to be particularly severe. The Secretary of State's proposal for licensed teachers is one measure which may assist the recruitment of teachers in the future, but urgent consideration also has to be given to the nature and quality of the on-the-job training provided both by LEAs and teacher training institutions if sufficient people of the right calibre are to be attracted and retained within the education service.

LEAs have a long way to go to meet the recommendations of the James Report on the induction and early in-service training of teachers. The introduction of grant related in-service training for teachers, greater specification of national priorities and the opportunity for LEAs to add their own local priorities has been helpful. In many authorities, there is increased emphasis on school-based curriculum review and the formulation of staff development policies as a means of achieving curriculum development with school focused in-service training to support that process. Many schools have designated professional tutors who will fulfil a most important staff development function, not only for newly qualified teachers, but also for teachers in mid-career. The increased call on teachers' time for school focused INSET in school hours has created major problems, particularly in the context of the determination of a teacher's directed time commitment of 1265 hours per annum. The shortage of teachers has led too to difficulties in many parts of the country in securing supply teachers to cover the absence of teachers from their classes on in-service training or a variety of other legitimate activities associated with their professional function in the school or college. Several authorities are giving consideration to alternative ways of providing resources for supply cover, particularly by the allocation of full-time, permanent posts to individual schools or groups of schools to enable them to manage the cover for absent teachers and at the same time to provide effective teaching for the students. The evaluation of such arrangements is particularly urgent in view of the need to resolve the matter satisfactorily for schools operating under local management arrangements.

The provision in the 1986 No. 2 Act for the Secretary of State to introduce a process of appraisal for teachers represents a further personnel management area for professional staffs in LEAs whether they are school or education office based. The process is at a relatively early stage in those schools and colleges where it has been introduced. Work through Education Support Grants in a number of authorities and the research undertaken in Suffolk, will be valuable to the profession in addressing the issue of the introduction of appraisal for teachers and has no doubt influenced the Secretary of State's thinking about the form of appraisal which he would wish to see introduced.

Good appraisal systems, to have the confidence of the staff involved, must have clear outcomes in terms of organizational and individual development and must be consistently and painstakingly operated. Anything less will be seen as a cosmetic exercise. Pressure on teacher time is a factor which needs to be resolved if appraisal systems in the schools and colleges are to be effective.

2. Education Officers and Advisers

A wealth of training opportunity is now available to Education Officers and advisers. The involvement of large consultancy organization in this field is of relatively recent date and is threatening to swamp the existing structures which have the confidence of Education Officers. The Management Development Committee of the Society of Education Officers has created a clear structure of staff and management development for Education Officers both at regional and national level. Introductory courses for new entrants to the profession, the 'main phase' course for experienced officers mounted in association with Sheffield Polytechnic, the advanced course for more experienced officers organized in association with INLOGOV and courses organized by the Society working jointly with the Local Government Training Board and the GRUBB institute are all highly valued by participants and Chief Education Officers. The opportunity for colleagues from different authorities to meet together away from their offices, and to share experiences under the guidance of experienced trainers and senior managers from Education Departments has proved successful in meeting the staff development needs of individual officers. The format is also used effectively to train staff in specific techniques or specialisms, an increasing need in these days of rapid change. Regional meetings of the Society of Education Officers and a large number of conferences and training opportunities provided by consultancies and agencies outside the education service contribute significantly to the great need for further training and information giving opportunities for managers in the education service.

There are many areas in which joint training between senior management staff in schools and Education Departments is necessary at the present time. A number of authorities find ways of organizing joint senior management training for heads, advisers and Education Officers, often in association with the more experienced consultancy groups. If Education Officers are to fulfil the important tasks presented by current and future legislation, continued attention will need to be given to the range, quality, accessibility and cost of relevant training opportunities in the future.

3. Manual, Clerical and Technician Staff

The general concept of development for non-teaching staff and support staff is equally vital, not only to ensure that staff are kept fully up-to-date on the effect of new legislation on their work and the introduction of new technology and systems of work, but also for updating and developing their personal and occupational skills. Local Authorities have provided courses over the years in a whole range of activities, notably health and safety courses and induction courses for new employees, and in the case of manual workers, courses for supervisors. School meals, caretaking and cleaning and grounds maintenance staff generally have training opportunities to develop the skills required to carry out their work efficiently. Administrative and clerical staff in Local Authorities usually have access to in-house and on-the-job training with opportunity for day release for qualification training. In many authorities, however, insufficient opportunity exists for institution-based clerical and administrative staff to pursue similar training opportunities. The efficient operation of schools in the changed circumstances following the implementation of the Education Reform Act will require hign level performance of such staff. Further attention needs to be given to identifying the continuing training needs of such staff and the best means of responding to them.

CONCLUSION

Senior staff in Education Authorities have achieved much in developing their personnel policies and practice since local government reorganization. Mechanisms are in place for effective consultation and negotiation with staff of the service although seldom in one forum. Procedures to deal with legislation introduced in the last fourteen years which impacts upon LEAs in their personnel management role, are soundly established and generally working well. Good working relationships have been built between education departments and central departments to ensure a consistent delivery of service to staff and through them to clients and there is clarity about the respective roles of central departments and education departments. Staff development programmes are well articulated, carefully planned and delivered and participation rates are increasing. More emphasis, however, needs to be given to joint staff development programmes for Education Officers, head teachers and advisers and there must be an improvement in provision for non-teaching staff who are institutionally based. Above all, education managers have demonstrated their ability to respond positively and effectively in a variety of ways to local manifestations of national problems in a period of increasingly rapid change. The service is in good shape to adapt its operations to cope with the particularly significant changes which are likely to impact upon its role as a result of the Education Reform Act.

Index